PROMOTIONAL ACTIVITY

www.smps.org

SMPS PUBLICATIONS is an imprint of the Society for Marketing Professional Services
123 N. Pitt Street, Suite 400, Alexandria, VA 22314

703.549.6117 | www.smps.org

SMPS is a not-for-profit, professional organization established to promote research and education that advances the body of knowledge in the field of professional services marketing and develops a greater understanding of the role and value of marketing in the A/E/C industry.

© 2016 by the Society for Marketing Professional Services (SMPS)®

SMPS is a registered service mark of the Society for Marketing Professional Services.

Cover Photo: Desert Bloom Porte Cochere at Morongo Casino Resort and Spa, Cabazon, CA.

© Paul Turang Photography / paulturang.com

Book design and layout: MilesHerndon / milesherndon.com

Domain 5: Promotional Activity

MARKENDIUM: SMPS Body of Knowledge

Library of Congress Control Number: 2016945980

ISBN-13: 978-0-9974818-1-5 (Paperback)

ISBN-13: 978-0-9974818-2-2 (EPUB)

10 9 8 7 6 5 4 3 2 1

Published in the United States of America

First Edition | First Printing

SMPS PUBLICATIONS are available for sale on most online retailers in the U.S., U.K., Canada and Australia. Books are also available to the trade through Ingram and Amazon.com. For more information, contact info@smps.org.

All rights reserved. No part of this book may be reprinted or reproduced or utilized in any form or by any electronic, mechanical or other means, now known or hereafter invented, including photocopying and recording, or in any information storage or retrieval system, without permission in writing from the Society for Marketing Professional Services (SMPS).

THE SOCIETY FOR MARKETING PROFESSIONAL SERVICES (SMPS) is a community of marketing and business development professionals working to secure profitable business relationships for their A/E/C companies. Through networking, business intelligence, and research, SMPS members gain a competitive advantage in positioning their firms successfully in the marketplace. SMPS offers members professional development, leadership opportunities, and marketing resources to advance their careers.

SMPS is the only organization dedicated to creating business opportunities in the A/E/C industry. Companies tap into a powerful national and regional network to form teams, secure business referrals and intelligence, and benchmark performance. SMPS was created in 1973 by a small group of professional services firm leaders who recognized the need to sharpen skills, pool resources, and work together to build their businesses.

Today, SMPS represents a dynamic network of approximately 6,700+ marketing and business development professionals from architectural, engineering, planning, interior design, construction, and specialty consulting firms located throughout the United States and Canada. The Society and its chapters benefit from the support of 3,700 design and building firms, encompassing 80 percent of the Engineering News-Record Top 500 Design Firms and Top 400 Contractors.

For more information, visit our website at:
www.smps.org

PUT THE DOMAINS TO WORK FOR YOU AND YOUR FIRM.

This comprehensive, six-book series further defines the six Domains of Practice for SMPS and the A/E/C community. Learn more at **smps.org/markendium** – and take your firm's marketing and business development efforts to the next level.

MARKENDIUM
SMPS BODY OF KNOWLEDGE

The MARKENDIUM: SMPS Body of Knowledge (BOK) is the premier go-to learning resource for the successful practice of marketing and business development in the A/E/C professions. The MARKENDIUM: BOK is not a singular publication or a catalog of ideas. It is inclusive of the contemporary knowledge necessary for thriving careers and firms in these professions and beyond.

The MARKENDIUM: BOK was curated in a collaborative way by experts in the A/E/C professions and is a compilation of existing and newly sourced content. The MARKENDIUM: BOK is built on the foundation of the six Domains of Practice identified by SMPS:

Marketing Research

Marketing Planning

Client and Business Development

Proposals

Promotional Activity

Management

Icon Legend

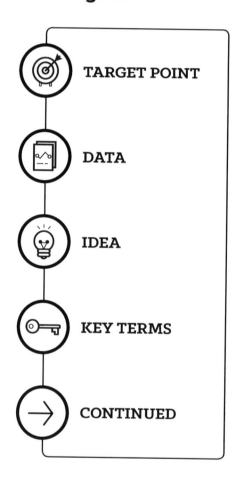

- TARGET POINT
- DATA
- IDEA
- KEY TERMS
- CONTINUED

Domain 5: Promotional Activity

Navigation Menu

Introduction		13
1	**Develop and Maintain Corporate Identity**	**14**
	1.1 Use Primary Research to Determine Brand Perception and Identity	14
	1.2 Develop a Vision and Mission Statement	15
	1.3 Develop a Unique Value Proposition	17
	1.4 Create an Identity Map	17
	1.4.1 Generalist vs Specialist	18
	1.4.2 Client Driven vs Market Driven	19
	1.4.3 Design vs Execution Focus	19
	1.4.4 Unique vs "Me Too" Player	19
	1.5 Determine Elements of a Corporate Identity Program	19
	1.5.1 Brand Architecture and Naming Conventions	19
	1.5.2 Graphic Design Elements	20
	1.5.3 Messaging	21
	1.6 Create Standards	22
	1.7 Key Terms	22
2	**Develop and Implement a Communications Plan**	**23**
	2.1 Develop a Communications Plan	23
	2.1.1 Define Your Communications Objectives	23
	2.1.2 Engage Firm Stakeholders	24
	2.1.3 Identify Key Topics	25
	2.1.4 Define Your Target Audience	25
	2.1.5 Create a Set of Communications Initiatives	28
	2.2 Develop a Social Media Plan	28
	2.2.1 Determine Target Audience and Goals for Each Platform	29

	2.2.2	Best Practices for Developing a Plan	33
	2.2.3	Track Progress, Determine Reach/Followers, and Track Return on Investment (ROI) Metrics	34
2.3	Maintain a Web Presence		34
	2.3.1	Determine Website Strategy	34
	2.3.2	Merging Current Systems with New Site's Structure	35
	2.3.3	Integration	36
	2.3.4	Benchmark Competitors' Websites	39
	2.3.5	Monitor and Manage Analytics	39
2.4	Key Terms		41

3 Media Relations — 42

3.1	Strategy and Planning		42
3.2	Maintain a Media List		42
	3.2.1	Research National Publications in Key Market Segments	42
	3.2.2	Local List	44
3.3	Draft News Releases		44
	3.3.1	Sample News Releases	46
	3.3.2	Assign Responsibility to In-House Staff or an Outside Consultant	47
3.4	Distribute Approved Release		47
3.5	Contacting the Media		48
	3.5.1	Follow-Up Protocols	49
3.6	Publish Newsletter or Journal Articles		49
	3.6.1	Choose a Topic	50
	3.6.2	Getting Published	51
	3.6.3	Determine the Communication Channel	52
3.7	Train Staff to Interact with Media		56
	3.7.1	Identify Personnel to Interact With the Press	56

	3.7.2 Training	56
	3.8 Key Terms	57
4	**Create Digital Content**	**58**
	4.1 Using Multimedia	58
	4.2 Videos	58
	4.2.1 Video Marketing	58
	4.2.2 Develop a Video Plan	63
	4.2.3 Legal Issues	65
	4.3 Audio Podcasts	65
	4.4 Key Terms	66
5	**Coordinate Photography**	**67**
	5.1 Develop a Plan that Aligns with Marketing, BD, and Strategic Plan Goals	67
	5.2 Identify Budget and Resources	68
	5.2.1 Photographing People	68
	5.2.2 Photographing Projects	70
	5.2.3 Stock Photos	71
	5.3 Elements of a Strong Photo	71
	5.3.1 Taking the Photos Yourself	74
	5.4 Best Practices for Working with Architectural Photographers	75
	5.5 Legal Issues	78
	5.6 Key Terms	79
6	**Prepare Award Competition Entries**	**80**
	6.1 Why Enter?	80
	6.2 Track Award Opportunities	81
	6.3 Determine Likelihood of Winning Award	81
	6.4 Include Visuals	82
	6.5 Include the Voice of the Client in the Award Narrative	83

		6.6	Budget Time and Resources for Editing, Proofing, Etc.	83
		6.7	Key Terms	83
7	**Develop an Advertising Plan**			**84**
	7.1	Establish an Advertising Rationale		84
	7.2	Relate Goals and Target Audience to Overall Marketing Plan		85
	7.3	Different Types of Ads and Sponsorships		87
		7.3.1	Institutional or Image Advertising	87
		7.3.2	Service Advertising	87
		7.3.3	Tombstone Advertisements	87
		7.3.4	Broadcast Advertising	88
		7.3.5	Advertorials	88
		7.3.6	Social Media Advertising	88
		7.3.7	PBS Underwriting	88
	7.4	Key Terms		89
8	**Plan Trade show Activities and Conference Speaking**			**90**
	8.1	Decide Whether to Participate		90
		8.1.1	Types of Trade shows/Conferences	90
		8.1.2	Align Your Goals with Trade show/Conference Opportunities	91
	8.2	Develop a Budget		93
	8.3	Craft a Plan of Engagement		93
		8.3.1	Choose Your Speaker's Topic	93
		8.3.2	Identify the Appropriate Participants for your Booth	94
		8.3.3	Constructing a Display	95
		8.3.4	Level of Presence	97
	8.4	Gather Information and Follow Up		97
	8.5	Evaluate ROI Post-Show		98
	8.6	Key Terms		99
9	**Coordinate Firm Special Events**			**100**

9.1	Plan the Event	100
	9.1.1 Define Your Goals	100
	9.1.2 Identify Your Audience	101
	9.1.3 Develop the Central Concept	102
	9.1.4 Give it the Creative Sparkle	102
9.2	Check, then Double Check	103
9.3	Post Event	104
9.4	Other Corporate Entertainment Strategies	104
9.5	Key Terms	106
10	**Select Vendors and Consultants**	**107**
	10.1 Define the Scope of Work	107
	10.2 Select and Interview Vendors and Consultants	108
	10.3 Manage and Direct Activities of Consultants	110
	10.4 Key Terms	111
11	**Case Study Activity**	**112**
12	**Glossary**	**115**
13	**Related Resources**	**122**
14	**Figures**	**123**
15	**Index**	**124**
16	**About the Photographer**	**128**
17	**Peer Review**	**128**
18	**Body of Knowledge Subject Matter Experts (SMEs)**	**129**

MARKENDIUM // **Domain 5:** Promotional Activity

PROMOTIONAL ACTIVITY

Introduction

MARKENDIUM: The SMPS body of knowledge for Professional Services Marketers is classified under six Domains of Practice. These Domains of Practice are as follows:

Domain 1: Marketing Research

Marketing research is executed to gather, record, and analyze data related to marketing a firm's services. The data can be used to identify and define marketing opportunities; generate, refine, and evaluate marketing actions; monitor marketing performance; and forecast trends.

Domain 2: Marketing Planning

The marketing plan serves as a map to define a firm's market prospects and key market characteristics. The plan should include marketing goals and strategies to ensure successful direction to the team, as well as information on how marketing budgets and efforts should be spent.

Domain 3: Client and Business Development

Business development involves relationship building with current and prospective clients, often prior to a request for proposal. Through interaction with the client, development activities may include calls, visits, correspondence, social media, referrals, and tradeshows.

Domain 4: Proposals

Proposals are prepared in response to a specific solicitation where the project and scope of work are identified. Proposals can include general firm information, relevant projects, a technical project approach, and key staff résumés.

Domain 5: Promotional Activity

This undertaking includes all forms of communications and inbound/outbound marketing. Some examples include advertising, direct mail, website, social media, brochures, presentations, special events, public relations, and news releases.

Domain 6: Management

Management involves coordinating the efforts of staff and/or consultants to accomplish marketing goals and objectives. Using available resources, management effectively plans, organizes, staffs, and directs projects of an organization or firm.

As mentioned above, this fifth Domain, Promotional Activity, covers all forms of marketing communications, including digital and social marketing. We'll start by discussing how to develop a corporate identity that creates a good first impression, and fosters continued client loyalty. We'll look at developing an effective communications plan, and how it works with social media and advertising to raise awareness of your company in the minds of prospective clients. We'll see how companies can create sophisticated audio and visual materials to get their targeted messages out via the Web, and we'll cover the continuing importance of photography to communications.

We'll discuss the use of consultants in promoting your business, and insights into winning awards competitions. And finally, we'll look into the rewards and pitfalls of event planning, and how special events can leave a favorable lasting impression with clients and potential clients.

1 Develop and Maintain Corporate Identity

Your brand is the face that your firm presents to your clients and to the world. Developing a corporate identity creates a good first impression, and fosters continued client loyalty. Using good design practices and consistent messaging reinforces the image that you want to project.

By the end of this section, you should understand the following key points, and be able to use them in your promotional activity work:

- The importance of branding on how your firm is perceived in the marketplace
- How to differentiate your company and create a unique value proposition
- How to use graphic design and messaging to create a strong corporate identity

1.1 Use Primary Research to Determine Brand Perception and Identity

A brand is more than a name or a logo, and "branding" is not just advertising, merchandising, or promotion. Your brand represents the perceptions that both internal and external audiences have of your firm; these perceptions can be formed from a single experience with your brand, such as the first time your logo is seen or your name is heard, or from multiple experiences over an extended period of time. Therefore, regardless of where or how your audiences experience your brand, it is important that your brand message is consistent, because consistency contributes to pattern recognition that is critical to building brand awareness and familiarity. These messages are your firm's identity, and include everything from a consistent color palette and logo to what values an employee emphasizes when she talks about her firm.

The principal role of a brand is to differentiate your firm from competitors. The strongest brands demonstrate differentiation in product and service offerings and in the way management and employees "live the brand" each day. Brand strategy should

support a firm's business strategy as well. Business goals and objectives are easier to achieve if the firm's branding is accurate, artful, and compelling. For example, Southwest Airlines' business strategy is to be a low-cost, no-frills airline. Yet, Southwest knows it must still provide a high level of individual client service to be successful in the long term. So the color schemes of their planes, zany advertising, and a culture of friendly, even playful, employees are communicating the idea of fun in addition to value.

Image and corporate identity can be within your control rather than left to chance. A firm's image program, like other types of marketing and promotional campaigns, needs to be strategically developed, executed, and sustained.

A good way to find out where you currently stand in terms of your firm's image is by conducting a perception survey. A perception survey is a series of questions posed to partners, clients, and employees that acquires the information that will be used to shape the company's identity program. It is the first step in determining how your brand is viewed by others. Some common questions asked in a perception survey include:

- What are some words that you would use to describe this company?
- What are some projects that this company has worked on?
- Describe a person who works in this company.

The results you receive can help you to determine whether other people's perception of your company lines up with the image that you want to project, and what areas of your brand you need to work on. If your firm works across multiple regions or markets, a perception survey can detect exactly where different geographic or sector-specific weaknesses exist.

1.2 Develop a Vision and Mission Statement

In addition to learning how others view you, figure out how you view yourself. What kind of firm are you? This isn't a simple question, as there is no finite number of answers, and it's important to be as specific as possible. "We're an engineering firm" isn't an answer that provides much information to guide your marketing efforts. But "We're a structural engineering firm that specializes in the most complex structures in the world" gives you a lot more to work with. So, how do you define who you are?

Engage internal stakeholders in the conversation. What do they believe is your firm's core purpose? The following questions can help you start:

- Who are we?
- Why do we exist?
- What makes us different from other firms?
- What do we want to be known for?

Your vision statement is an expression of what your firm aspires to be. This is the place to use superlatives: best, leading, largest, most, finest. In your wildest fantasies, what is your firm all about? Design? Innovation? Efficiency? Service? How does your work improve the lives of your clients? How does your firm change the world for the better with every project? A vision statement could be something like this:

> AB&C is a design firm that improves the lives of hospital patients and medical professionals by taking a fresh look at healthcare design and applying the best practices from around the world to our projects.

Try to express your vision statement as concisely as possible. Write it out first and allow it to be as long as it needs to be, and then cut things that aren't critical. Try to get it down to one key idea. Make it as active and as ambitious as possible. Here's an even better vision statement:

> DE&F designs the most successful hotel and resort properties in the world.

It can be very challenging to write a statement like this in a group. You may not get to your final answer in the discussion, but try anyway. Begin with a blank piece of paper. Ask the group to throw out words that describe what they think the firm is, at heart, all about—not the realistic, earthbound stuff, but the truly aspirational and inspirational. How do you impact the world?

Once the ideas start rolling, you'll be able to see which ones rise to the top. After you've accumulated enough raw material, prompt the group to pick what they think the absolutely most important things are; then take a pass at writing down the vision statement. Ask the group to edit it. Move on when you feel that you've accomplished all you can in the meeting. You may need to rework it after the meeting and send it out later for the group to review.

A mission statement is much more directed than the vision statement. It describes not who you are as a firm, but where the firm is going. It describes how you plan to change your practice—not the world. Think big, but create a mission that is practical and achievable. Here's a sample mission statement:

> We intend to transform our company into the most respected laboratory design firm on the West Coast. We will accomplish this by hiring the best staff, rigorously improving the quality and accuracy of our design, and delivering on our promises.

TARGET POINT

Start developing your mission statement by asking the question, "Where do we want to go now?" Is there an existing market that you'd like to penetrate further? Is there an area of your practice that you'd like to improve?

Just as with the vision statement, recognize that you may not be able to complete the mission statement while you're in the meeting. Everybody may need to give it some thought. Let it go when you feel that you've gone as far as you can. Remember that what's most important isn't producing a neat and tidy plan, but the process of working together with the key minds in your firm to discuss and reach agreement on key issues.

1.3 Develop a Unique Value Proposition

Your unique value proposition is what sets you apart from your competition. It's a short statement—only one or two sentences—that tells prospective clients your area of expertise and what they'll get when they hire you.

Today's A/E/C industry is, in many venues, characterized as a commodity market—there are many providers who all tend to look alike, so price often plays a powerful role in the selection decision. Therefore, when establishing your unique value proposition, the client's perception of your unique value holds the most weight. Seek out their opinions, and listen to what they say without trying to lead the conversation. Even if you disagree with them, or think they're misinterpreting an aspect of your business, this will give you information on how your company is perceived from the outside and is valid because it influences whether clients will want to choose you to do business with. If what they say doesn't align with how your perceive yourself—even if their assumptions are simply not true—knowing what they think allows you to tailor your marketing efforts to fix any misperceptions.

Differentiation is more of an internal issue, and one that you have more influence over than your perceived value to a client or sector. If you haven't done one in a while, perform a SWOT analysis, paying special attention to the items in each category that are unique to you and your company. SWOT stands for the strengths and weaknesses of your firm, and the opportunities and threats that face it due to external forces. The strengths and weaknesses are about the internal workings of your firm. Brainstorm what aspects of your product or service (including client service) differentiate you from your competitors. For more information about how to conduct a SWOT analysis, see Domain 2.

In order to know how you stand out from your competitors, you must first identify and learn about them. What markets do they operate within? Where is their home office, and where do they have regional/satellite offices? What are their service offerings? What are their strengths?

Say you find that one of your competitors offers something they call "design-build," which is the same service you offer. Find out more about their service—how is it different from yours? Do you use a different technology or software? Maybe your team has more expertise than theirs—for example, someone who has designed more stadiums than any other person, or whose recent high school design is considered the latest and greatest in the field.

Above all, be honest—with yourself and with your clients. Your unique value proposition is not what you want your company to be; it's what it is right now. It's a promise to your client that you have to be able to deliver. Choose opportunities that your firm's unique abilities will enable you to excel in, and you'll be more likely to build a strong client base and attract more of the right type of clients for your business.

1.4 Create an Identity Map

In your discussion about your firm's unique strengths, feel free to talk about other firms as models or benchmarks. "We're like Big Firm A, but we're smaller and more focused." "We're like Small Design Firm B, but our design style is more driven by the client than our own tastes." These comparisons help you to categorize your firm and to figure out where you fit within the solar system of your competitors.

An identity map is a great tool for exploring how you compare with your competitors. Select two factors and map one on the X-axis and one on the Y-axis. (This example uses size and generalist/specialist as the two factors.) Put your competitors on the map and put your own firm on the map, in order to establish a common understanding of how you compare.

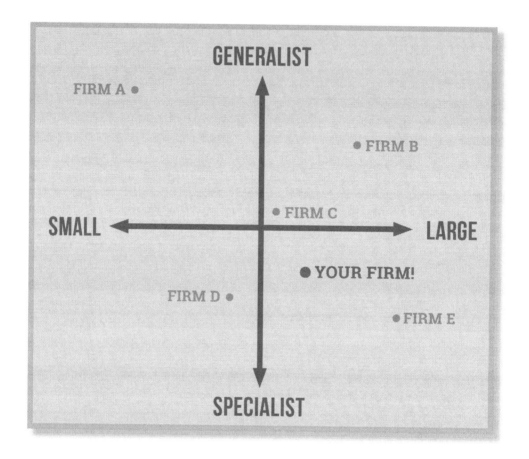

Figure 1.1 - Identity Map (Marketing Handbook)

You may want to use the following factors to create an identity map (either as the X-axis or Y-axis) or just talk about them with your firm's leaders.

1.4.1 Generalist vs. Specialist

There are advantages and disadvantages to the strategies of being a generalist or a

niche specialist. A strategy of generalization, of pursuing work in a number of markets, can enable the firm to grow through pursuing new kinds of work and is often more stable, as the downturns in one market may be offset by opportunities in others. A strategy of specialization, of pursuing work in one or just a few markets, while not usually enabling the kind of growth or long-term stability of the generalist strategy, can be incredibly profitable. If your firm "owns" a market—that is, you're the obvious leader in that area—a lot less time and money are required to bring in new work, and your firm's profitability can soar.

1.4.2 Client Driven vs. Market Driven

Some firms grow by focusing on a limited number of existing clients and seeking new opportunities to provide services to these clients. Other firms focus less on existing clients, but may focus on growing through increased penetration of one or more markets. Truly successful firms do both of these well—servicing existing clients and gaining a majority of their work through repeat business, while growing by acquiring new clients in markets in which the firm has some expertise.

1.4.3 Design vs. Execution Focus

Depending on whether you are an architect, an engineer, a specialty consultant, or a contractor, you may view your firm as being more concerned with design (the big idea, the vision, providing the solution to the client's challenges) or execution (completing the project successfully in a way that meets the client's expectations with few surprises and minimized risk). Clearly, some large firms try to emphasize both design and execution. But it can be an important anchoring question to discuss with your firm's leaders whether they see themselves as more about design or more about execution.

1.4.4 Unique vs. "Me Too" Player

What makes you special? Are you a unique firm, with a distinctive approach or perspective, or do you see your firm as being one of the pack?

1.5 Determine Elements of a Corporate Identity Program

Once you've conducted primary research and developed a core purpose, it's time to focus on the more specific elements that will represent the outcome of your corporate identity program. These are the items that are more changeable over time. Your corporate identity should be refreshed through large initiatives every five to ten years, but the items covered within the categories below will likely change more frequently based on your overall marketing plan.

1.5.1 Brand Architecture and Naming Conventions

Brand architecture defines the relationship and hierarchy of the firm's parent brand to a firm's sub-brands, divisions, departments, joint ventures, and affiliations.

Management of these relationships and their hierarchy helps the firm clearly define its offerings. Without proper brand architecture, a firm can appear schizophrenic. Not only does this unnecessary confusion dampen the enthusiasm for a firm's products and services, it is inconsistent with the architecture engineering, and construction, industries, which promote precision and attention to detail.

Naming conventions establish structure and boundaries for all naming needs within a firm. Structure ensures consistency both visually and verbally. Boundaries set the criteria and latitude for name development creativity.

Brand architecture and naming conventions work together to ensure clean, crisp communication of a firm's moving parts. These tools save time when a new entity, product, or service is added, and substantially increase the cumulative effect of marketing expenditures.

A variety of brand architecture schemes are common. A monolithic architecture uses one name for the branding of all entities. A dominant architecture uses one brand as the lead brand with subordinate entities identified in the descriptive modifier. A logo-linked architecture can have multiple brands that share the same symbol. Discrete architecture means that every brand is different. Cobranding is often used in partnerships or affiliations. Endorsed branding means that separate brand names are endorsed by typically one other brand. As organizational complexity, product proliferation, global expansion, and other forces creep into the mix, a blend of two or more schemes is becoming important.

A blended solution can be difficult to develop and manage. This difficulty is diminished by consulting with professionals who regularly create "brand architecture decision tools" that provide criteria for decision making. Also, having a decision tool reduces internal political resistance to change, since an approved firm-wide tool mitigates any particular entity or department thinking that they are the only one being asked to modify their identity.

Each scheme has its strengths and weaknesses. Of all brand management tools, brand architecture is the most complex to learn, execute, and build consensus around, since development of various brand architecture models is mastered through hands-on experience. The only way to master the skill level required for complex, blended brand architecture schemes is to work with business factors and market appeal factors gathered over an extended period of time in many different industries. R. Harish's Brand Architecture: Concepts and Cases is one of the few books on this subject. See the Related Resources section for more information.

1.5.2 Graphic Design Elements

Design systems are created to promote a brand's positioning. Cookie-cutter design systems tire easily among a firm's designers, agencies, and clients. Flexibility should be built into the look and feel of print and digital communications design so that communications stay fresh, but the firm maintains a family look for all internal and external applications. Building in flexibility is more difficult than using cookie-cutter systems, since the graphic standards for creative development must be well-conceived and documentation must be very comprehensive. Design systems and graphic standards can be in a printed manual or placed on a password-protected Intranet.

In-house graphic designers may be concerned about having a design system and graphic standards; because they may feel that it will inhibit their creativity. Designers with true corporate identity experience, or those who have an open mind, know that the opposite is true. Brand management should draw a clear distinction between design for art's sake vs. corporate identity and brand-building for the sake of the business; because if a firm's print and digital applications are inconsistent, the firm's brand message is less effective and marketing dollars are being wasted.

At a minimum, a design system should include a statement of purpose, why graphic standards matter, and an agreement to follow the standards. Also, the following signature standards should be addressed: clear space, staging, sizing, color, color options, and misuse of brand elements.

Other graphic design elements that you should make sure are aligned with your corporate identity:

- Logo
- Typography
- Corporate and support colors
- Imagery (e.g., type of photography used)
- Placement of messaging (e.g., where the tagline should appear)

1.5.3 Messaging

A message platform builds out the brand positioning by identifying individual target audiences, identifying which attributes in the firm's brand positioning are the most compelling for each audience, and then providing appropriate "proof points."

Proof points are words or phrases that give the specific audience permission to believe the firm's assertion. As an example, if a hospital's brand positioning is based upon high tech, then high tech communications need to vary by audience. When communicating to patients, the hospital may say that high tech means less-invasive surgery with robotics and lower rates of infection; for nurse recruiting ads, the hospital may say that high tech means electronic medical records and less paperwork; for insurance companies, the hospital may say that high tech means faster diagnosis and fewer days off from work, reducing insurance costs; when communicating to donors, high tech may mean a healthier community in which the donor lives.

A message platform is akin to bending the brand positioning without breaking it. Bending is especially important when the audience is very diverse and/or a firm's product and service offerings are very different. Once conceived, a message platform essentially documents the DNA of a brand and is a referral resource for most, if not all, marketing and public relations (PR) communications initiatives. It creates a common vocabulary that allows everyone in the firm to use one language to talk about what you are, what you do, and how you do it.

1.6 Create Standards

Your brand represents the perceptions that both internal and external audiences have of your firm. By creating and enforcing standards around how your brand is presented, you have a better chance of shaping the perceptions that different audiences will have of your brand. Standards will help your brand send consistent messages; consistency contributes to the pattern recognition that is critical to building brand awareness and familiarity.

In order to ensure consistency, make sure that new content passes the brand test and will contribute to building your brand rather than detracting from it. Create a brand manual that outlines how to use (and how not to use) the company logo and associated elements of your corporate identity, and educate employees on its use.

Corporate identity guidelines can differ greatly depending on the size of the organization. Some outline incredibly specific instructions for every minute design aspect of everything from business cards to Microsoft PowerPoint presentations, while others are more lenient (providing just a specific Pantone color logo and template for a news release, for example). A collection showing different levels of identity guidelines can be found in the Related Resources section.

1.7 Key Terms

Below are the main terms covered in this section:
- Brand
- Differentiation
- Corporate identity
- Perception survey
- Vision statement
- Mission statement
- Unique value proposition
- Value
- Strengths, Weaknesses, Opportunities, and Threats (SWOT) analysis
- Identity map
- Brand architecture
- Naming conventions
- Proof points
- Corporate identity guidelines
- Image

2 Develop and Implement a Communications Plan

The messages that you communicate to current and prospective clients need to be consistent with your corporate vision, and advance your overall marketing goals. To be effective, your communications plan should encompass several different mediums, many of which are further discussed in this Domain (i.e., social media, advertising, blogs, publications, etc.).

By the end of this section, you should understand the following key points, and be able to use them in your promotional activity work:

- The importance of a clearly defined, goal-oriented communications plan
- The growing role and utilization of various mediums in corporate messaging
- How to measure the effectiveness of your corporate communications program

2.1 Develop a Communications Plan

A communications plan is an essential part of your marketing program and should not be overlooked. This document can help you to identify what characteristics of your company will appeal to a prospective client as well as to partners, potential employees, and even existing employees. A well-developed communications plan targets your audience in detail and identifies the medium best suited to communicate the message. Ultimately, it engages the audience and inspires them to take an interest in your firm.

The communications plan will also help you to establish measurable goals. You will be able to define, in concrete terms, whether or not your marketing communications program is working. Moreover, it helps you establish consistency in all of your marketing efforts. Once you determine what messages you must communicate and to whom, you can make sure that all of your marketing efforts will work in concert with one another to generate the results that you want.

2.1.1 Define Your Communications Objectives

The communications plan is an extension of the company's strategic and marketing plans. Strategic objectives developed in these plans set the priorities and direction for communicating with clients, potential clients, the community, and other key audiences. They define where you want to be within a given time period. Based on the goals and objectives in these plans, identifying the goals of the communications plan should be a straightforward task. The following are some examples of marketing goals:

- Enter a new geographic area and generate $1 million in fees in the coming 24 months
- Introduce a new product or service to the marketplace in the coming year
- Increase market share by five percent more than the past year
- Generate a 50/50 mix of bid and negotiated work within the next two years
- Become known as an expert in your field within the next 15 months

From these goals, you should establish clear-cut communications objectives—the responses that you desire from your target audience. Develop as many communications objectives as possible for each marketing goal. For instance, if your goal is to enter a new geographic area and generate $1 million in fees within the next 24 months, you might establish the following objectives:

- Create awareness of your company in the new geographic area
- Create awareness of your product or service in the new geographic area
- Generate a following for your company in the new geographic area
- Develop thought leadership of your product or service in the new geographic area

You will notice that each of these communications objectives works with marketing goals to create conversation about the product or service.

In addition to helping you decide what you must do to accomplish your goals, communications objectives help you to measure your results, to determine how well you have accomplished each objective, and to decide whether the money you spent on marketing generated the results you expected. Your objectives will help you to isolate which parts of your communications plan are working and which are not.

Measuring results is not as easy as determining whether or not your goals have been met. If your goal was to enter a new market and generate $1 million in revenue within 24 months and you failed to do so, it is not necessarily the fault of your communications plan. Variables not controlled by the communications plan—such as price, quality, the ability of your sales staff, and general economic conditions—may all contribute to your results. There may be market conditions, national crises, or international events that have affected everyone's business and that you could not possibly have factored into your plan.

What you can measure instead is whether you have met your communications objectives. Have you established awareness? Have you established a liking or preference for your firm? To measure how well you create awareness of your company or your competitive advantages, you might conduct a random survey of prospective clients before the marketing communications campaign begins and measure the percentage of your target audience that is aware of your company.

After implementing your communications plan, you should conduct another random survey of a similar number of prospective clients to measure the percentage that is aware of your company and its services or products. Surveys can also measure whether your campaign has established liking or preference for your product or service. And, of course, if your objective is to generate responses, you can easily determine the number of responses in a given time period before and after your campaign.

2.1.2 Engage Firm Stakeholders

If there is no data or research on what your clients want or need to know, it will be necessary to do some digging in order to further define your objectives. Consider a

client research initiative or survey to gain additional insight into client issues, needs, and opportunities.

IDEA
Don't forget your in-house resources! Gather reliable data and anecdotal evidence from internal staff with client-facing roles. Be sure to document what you collect.

An excellent source of secondary research about your clients is the professional associations to which they belong. Professional associations often produce research on what is of urgent interest to members. For example, many higher education clients are facing a significant demographic issue today with declining enrollment and the increasing competition for the smaller pool of potential students. Addressing this issue with knowledge and research on what students and their parents expect for facilities and services on campus can be a powerful strategy. The data and survey information produced by a higher education association or publication will inform this strategy.

2.1.3 Identify Key Topics

Based on your firm's strategic and marketing plans, it is important to begin identifying key topics that the communications plan will address. These could be differentiators or unique value propositions (as discussed in section 1), and they will become the backbone of your communications plan.

2.1.4 Define Your Target Audience

Once you have established your goals and objectives and identified key topics, you need to determine your target audience. For example, this may be the group of people most likely to buy your products or services. Note the words, "most likely to buy." Your target audience is not every potential buyer, but rather those who would benefit most from your particular products or services and who would respond best to your competitive advantages.

You probably have more than one target audience, so it's a good idea to prioritize the groups in terms of primary, secondary, and so on. This will help you to allocate your resources, concentrating most of your time and money on reaching the primary target audience.

An audience is defined by its demographic and psychographic characteristics. Demographic characteristics are those that can be measured or quantified. They include characteristics like business type, geographic location, number of employees, annual revenue, and even specific job titles within the organization. Demographic characteristics are relatively easy to identify.

Psychographic characteristics group people into homogenous segments based on their psychological makeup and lifestyles. They might include factors like interests, hobbies, beliefs, and so on. Although psychographic characteristics are more difficult to define, they are often more important than demographic ones. Purchasing decisions, even those made by businesspeople, are based on how a product can satisfy the buyer's needs. Understanding prospective buyers' psychographic traits will help you to understand their needs and how your product or service can satisfy those needs.

When first defining your target audience, start with broad definitions. If you are an interior architect, perhaps your primary target audience will be space users. Your secondary target audience may be building owners because they often have some influence in the selection of an interior architect. Further, you may feel that commercial brokers, property managers, developers, and even interior general contractors might compose your tertiary target market.

Once you have decided what type of people will fall within your target markets, you should narrow your definition to best suit your particular competitive advantages. Start with their demographic characteristics. See the story below for a demonstration of how a firm might navigate this process.

TARGET POINT
Staying on Target

ABC is an interior architecture firm with a special knack for designing office interiors that are between 1,000 and 20,000 square feet. Since ABC is a small firm and doesn't have the resources to prepare quantities of proposals, they only want to pursue negotiated projects. They have also narrowed their geographic scope to a 50-mile radius of their office in Tulsa in order to provide the best level of service. With these specifics in mind, they turned to Emanuel, one of their marketers, to figure out what audiences they should target.

Over the weekend, Emanuel talked to his friend, a broker, and asked how many square feet of office space a typical employee occupies. She answered that when you factor in common areas, each employee uses about 200 square feet. With a little math, Emanuel figured out that this meant that ABC would do their best work for companies that have between five and 100 employees.

In order to further narrow ABC's primary target audience, Emanuel makes the assumption that a principal or office manager in each of these companies would be the one making decisions about hiring an interior architect. He realizes that there are more principals than office managers at the smaller firms, and decides to target these firms. He reasons that inquiries sent to principals will be forwarded to someone with responsibility for hiring architectural firms.

Because ABC has decided to pursue negotiated work, Emanuel can eliminate certain types of businesses, such as government agencies. He is also able to identify specific counties or towns to target since ABC has narrowed their geographic range to a 50-

mile radius. In this way, Emanuel has found the demographic profile of his primary target audience:

- Office space users
- Private sector companies with between five and 100 employees
- People with the title of principal
- Companies in the nearest three counties

The secondary and tertiary target audiences can be narrowed down in the same manner. Since the firm's secondary target audience consists of building owners, Emanuel narrows his list of owners to those whose buildings would have space in those nearest three counties.

Emanuel realizes, however, that there is more than one decision-maker in each firm, so he decides to include all of the principals in each firm. He figures that if they later realize that the total number of owners is too large to reasonably pursue, ABC can narrow its audience to only the senior principals.

The tertiary target audience is the commercial brokerage companies in those counties. Emanuel follows a similar logic in deciding who to pursue.

When he's done, the demographic profile of his secondary and tertiary audience looks like this:

Secondary
- Building owners
- All principals within those firms
- Companies in the three nearest counties

Tertiary
- Commercial brokerage companies
- All brokers in those companies
- Commercial real estate developers
- Project management positions in those companies
- Interior general contractors
- Estimators in those companies
- Project managers in those companies

Key Concepts for this Story:
- Clearly understand your company's strengths and limitations
- Develop a rationale for narrowing the focus of your targeting efforts
- Gather as much data as possible to support your conclusions
- Analyze your data carefully before making a decision about how best to apply your company's strengths to going after the primary target audience

Narrowing your target audience in this way is important for at least two reasons. First, it keeps you from wasting your time chasing prospective clients who may not be a good match for your services. Second, when it comes time to develop or purchase a list of prospects, you have quantifiable parameters that a list seller can use to build a list for you.

Once you have a clear understanding of your target audience in demographic terms, you should attempt to determine their psychographic characteristics. People buy the benefits derived from a service. Sometimes those benefits are emotional, like stress reduction, but more often than not the benefits are business details, such as saving time or money.

In this manner, it is possible to develop a loose description of the psychographic characteristics of your target audience based upon your competitive advantages. If you feel that your honest dealings with clients and your high level of client service are your strengths, then your target audience's psychographic characteristics might include an appreciation for being taken care of by someone who is straightforward. Although you will not find such details when purchasing lists, you can learn any pertinent details about your target audience through your own research. Knowing your target audience's psychographic characteristics will help you to find the best language with which to communicate to them.

2.1.5 Create a Set of Communications Initiatives

We'll spend the rest of this Domain discussing different communications initiatives (e.g., advertising, social media, websites, blogs, etc.), so this paragraph will contain only an overview of what to consider when creating a set of communications initiatives. Each of the following points will be discussed in more detail later:

- Match the initiative with your marketing plan in order to meet strategic objectives. What initiatives, done how often, on what topics, and written by whom, will get the response you desire?
- Support these initiatives with specific targets based on client sector and need.
- Create a content calendar that highlights your firm's strengths and times specific content to be released in conjunction with appropriate events, such as firm project milestones, conference appearances or awards won.
- Test the effectiveness of digital and social channels by monitoring engagement with clients and tracking the frequency that clients share, like, "favorite," or respond to your content.
- Assign individual author, editor and production roles with timelines using a content calendar.

2.2 Develop a Social Media Plan

Social media platforms such as LinkedIn, Twitter and Facebook are effective at driving

traffic to other online destinations such as blogs, articles and videos. A variety of social media platforms exist to help companies share content and connect with audiences, and different members of your audience will use different tools. Firms should use social and digital platforms appropriate to their audiences, and should integrate tools and share content in multiple ways:

- Determine which platforms are the best to use based on your audience and your goals; don't just jump on the newest ones.
- Professional social media profiles provide an online presence for your staff and another opportunity to showcase their expertise.
- Develop best practices and share them with your company to help them use social media intelligently and effectively.
- Make sure that your firm leaders and sector experts are visible on and knowledgeable about social networking sites.
- Take time to organize and use dashboards and programs that allow you to create lists of connections whose updates you don't want to miss.
- Track/monitor what is being posted or reported about your company and your clients.
- Review the various social media outlets that your competitors are using, what they are covering on those sites, etc.
- Social media is an excellent listening tool. In addition to sharing content, read content shared by your audience members. Converse with your connections so that you stay at the top of their mind and make them feel appreciated and listened to.

Inbound marketing—the practice of participating in a dialogue with clients through social media, content sharing and other tools—is the future. This type of back and forth allows clients to come to you on their own terms, and demonstrates the value that you can offer them by providing valuable information. This stands in opposition to traditional outbound methods (such as cold calling and direct mailing) that are static and concentrate on your firm instead of on the client.

With this increasing preference toward interactive marketing, you need to participate in the online conversation at the heart of social media. Take it one step beyond simply finding, following and developing your own online resources for others to find. Contributing well-crafted comments, posted by a CEO or sector experts, can pay-off in unexpected ways. You will be seen by more clients and influencers than the firm reaches in a whole year of outbound marketing (the traditional ad campaigns of yore), and you can create a following for the firm and posting "expert" that ends up steering business your way.

2.2.1 Determine Target Audience and Goals for Each Platform

As with any other plan, it is essential to ensure that your social media program supports your firm's overall goals. Review the strategic and marketing plan before creating goals specifically for your social media program.

Set your goals based on measurable data. In social media, this means number of reposts, retweets, comments, followers and new website visits. Use monitoring software, such as Hootsuite, to read social and digital activity, and to see how an action (e.g., a post, a tweet, etc.) affects your numbers. Adjust your plan based on that information.

Developing a numerical goal can be challenging, as each firm's goals will vary widely depending on its client and market sectors. Some firms have niche audiences, and consequently may expect to hear from only one or two clients within the time period, while a firm with big, global audiences wants to see its content shared by hundreds (or thousands) of people. The ultimate goal for measurement is to see an increase in requests for proposals (RFPs), client inquiries and opportunities, recruiting, and evidence of other responses to thought leadership.

Each social media platform has a slightly different audience and tone, and social media should be tailored to match the goals set. Research the audience demographics and growth projects of different social media channels. The table below gives an overview of the advantages and challenges of the most popular platforms.

Social Platform	Advantages	Key Metrics and Best Practices
Company Blog	<ul><li>Ideal method of establishing and reinforcing thought leader position</li><li>Can link audiences to blog from other social media</li><li>Option for using video and images</li><li>Opportunity for more personal and informal dialogue</li></ul>	<ul><li>Number of posts</li><li>Growth of subscribers and/or unique and return readers</li><li>Number of social shares</li><li>SEO improvement</li><li>Keep a consistent voice and style</li><li>Promote using other social channels</li><li>Avoid the "all-about-us" syndrome</li><li>Promote the channel to drive traffic</li></ul>
Twitter	<ul><li>Immediacy, simplicity of use, transparency, popularity</li><li>Audience interactivity via following, "favoriting" and retweeting</li><li>Ability to listen and respond to online conversations</li><li>Ability to be found and followed by editors, online journalists, bloggers and other influencers</li><li>Ability to follow and share content posted by clients</li></ul>	<ul><li>Number of posts</li><li>Number of followers; success with retweets and favorited tweets</li><li>Lead generation via monitoring</li><li>Referred traffic from tweeted links</li><li>Create a consistent voice for posts</li><li>Develop a strategy for Twitter engagement and differentiation</li><li>Segment influencers, clients, and journalists and create lists</li><li>Maintain daily monitoring and fast response to direct tweets and relevant mentions</li><li>Promote the channel to drive traffic</li></ul>
YouTube/Vimeo	<ul><li>Video becoming preferred method of content delivery and sharing</li><li>Ability to visually capture the personality, culture and stories of any organization</li><li>Versatility of use: media outreach, website content, presentations and firm's YouTube or Vimeo channel</li><li>Easily tracked viewing and sharing</li></ul>	<ul><li>Number of views</li><li>Number of shares</li><li>Referred traffic to firm website</li><li>SEO success from key terms</li><li>Determine level and quality of video production for desired audience</li><li>Keep videos short enough for online viewer to maintain interest</li><li>Involve clients in creating/sharing</li><li>Promote the channel to drive traffic</li></ul>
LinkedIn	<ul><li>Ability to share relevant content: news, blog posts, links and images</li><li>Ease of finding individual clients and decision-makers, and ease of them finding the firm</li><li>Ability to join and become a contributor to LinkedIn groups followed by clients and influencers</li><li>Ease of extending personal network and staying in touch with past clients</li><li>Ability to follow clients and share or comment on their content</li><li>Recruit talent</li></ul>	<ul><li>Number of posts</li><li>Page follows</li><li>Comments, likes, and shares</li><li>Group participation/dialogue</li><li>Assign responsibility for tracking LinkedIn activity in key groups</li><li>Follow the high volume of updates and postings</li><li>Educate all staff on how to use LinkedIn for business purposes</li><li>Promote the channel to drive traffic</li></ul>
Instagram	<ul><li>Real-time showcasing of visual content, events and celebrations</li><li>Ability to link back to website, blog and client assets</li><li>Opportunity to produce a series on a project or company initiative</li><li>More personal and immediate than some other social media channels</li><li>Opportunity for employees to participate by sharing project progress photos</li></ul>	<ul><li>Views, shares, and comments</li><li>Referral traffic</li><li>Inquiries or lead generation</li><li>SEO success from key terms</li><li>Determine oversight/ownership of Instagram site and content approval</li><li>Develop standards and image guidelines aligned with firm brand</li><li>Promote the channel to drive traffic</li></ul>
Facebook	<ul><li>Share a wide variety of videos, photos, news, links and content</li><li>Engage with employees, potential future employees, peer professionals adjacent organizations/companies and clients</li><li>Promote upcoming events/speaking appearances</li><li>Share social and community involvement side of company</li></ul>	<ul><li>Likes, shares, and company page follows</li><li>Engagement, reviews and comments</li><li>Traffic referred to other social sites</li><li>Decide if Facebook is matched to your target audiences; may be built for employee information-sharing</li><li>Develop standards for suitable content and assign oversight and approval responsibility</li><li>Promote the channel to drive traffic</li></ul>

Figure 2.1 - Social Media Platforms (provided by Mike Reilly)

2.2.2 Best Practices for Developing a Plan

When starting out, it's best to select just one or two social channels to engage with in order to avoid over-reaching and over-committing. Creating content and keeping up an online dialogue takes time! Platforms that mimic a real-time conversation, such as Facebook and Twitter, are especially draining because they require near-instantaneous responses.

Develop a strategy and content calendar for each platform. Scheduling your posts in advance allows you to choose your messaging more carefully and avoid having to constantly update a platform throughout the day. A content calendar is a framework for you to outline all of the types of content that you will produce over a period of time. A content calendar can include:

- Goals of the content you'll share
- Topics for the content
- Properties of each type of content (Who are you targeting? What brand attributes of your firm are you focusing on?)
- Authors of the content
- Distribution (Where will the content be distributed? A blog? An article pitch? An industry conference?)
- Deadlines and publication dates

Once you lay out all of the content and break it into regular intervals, it feels a lot more manageable. Including all of the content that you'll produce in one calendar helps you to keep an eye on both internal and external deadlines (like calls for presentations and your internal blog, for example). It helps you to see opportunities for integration and re-use of topics.

Here are a few other key actions that you should make sure to include in the development of any plan:

- Find the knowledge and information within your firm that will best demonstrate your value
- Translate that value and report it in a way that is interesting, educational, and entertaining to your audience
- Wherever possible, tie information about your company's actions into current events and social/cultural trends

A/E/C is a business-to-business industry, which means that a firm's knowledge is its main product. The sourcing and sharing of that knowledge is therefore the most important practice in a marketing activity. Find interesting content within your organization and translate that knowledge in a way that fits the social and digital channels that you decide to use.

Because social media operates in real time (as opposed to analog publications, where there is a lag between submittal and viewership), you have the opportunity to connect

your social media to other real-time events. If, for example, the EPA has just released a big report on global warming, you can incorporate that news event into a piece on your social media account about the importance of being sustainable. Make your posts relevant to what's going on in the world and you will draw in much more interest.

2.2.3 Track Progress, Determine Reach/Followers, and Track Return on Investment (ROI) Metrics

We mentioned Hootsuite as a good monitoring software program already, and later in this section we will discuss Google Analytics—both are good ways to track return on investment (ROI) metrics related to social media. These are only two of the many services available to help you to figure out how well you're reaching your followers through different platforms. Basic abilities, such as tracking how many followers you have, are free, whereas other services cost money. If you want to know how many times someone comments on videos you post related to a particular healthcare project, for example, you'll need to really drill down. It is important to determine what services are right for you based on what your goals are, what your social media plan is, and what your expectations are in terms of ROI over time.

See the Related Resources section for a list of different monitoring tools.

2.3 Maintain a Web Presence

Developing and maintaining a credible web presence is as much an art as a science. Josh Miles of MilesHerndon, an Indianapolis company specializing in branding strategy and digital marketing, stresses the importance of developing a website strategy, and tying it in to the overall marketing and business objectives of the company.

2.3.1 Determine Website Strategy

The first thing that you should consider when sitting down to develop your firm's website strategy is what you want the site to accomplish. Review your strategic plan and marketing goals in order to develop objectives for your site. Who is the audience(s) for your website?

One objective that firms today are focusing on is recruitment. So many firms are fighting for talent, trying to attract the best people, that recruitment is often considered a website's second—or even first—most important role. For firms with that goal, their target audience will primarily be job-seekers.

In order to attract people to your company, your website must represent your firm's culture. An entrepreneurial, young firm might pride itself on its willingness to try new technologies and push the envelope, but a job hunter wouldn't discover any of that if the firm's website is stuffy and static. Your web presence is a huge opportunity to express and build your firm's brand. Make sure that your website sends the same message through all of its elements—content, design, incorporation of social media, color schemes, etc.—and make sure that that message is in line with your brand. (For more on developing your brand, go back to section 1.)

The development of key messages has nothing to do with technology. In fact, it's a concern as old as time: How is your firm different? Think about the last time that you were shopping for an item online. You probably did a search, clicked the first link, and spent about two seconds determining if this site had the item that you were searching for. One, two ... back button. Does your current website pass the two-second test? And if so, once you begin to dig in to the content, does it position your firm differently than your competition?

2.3.2 Merging Current Systems with New Site's Structure

Even if you're conducting a major overhaul of a website that your firm hasn't updated since the early 2000s, it's likely that at least some of the information is still relevant to your firm's vision. Dig through whatever you have online already and determine what pages to keep, which to scrap, which to rework. From there, think about what new pages or features should be created to align with your strategic, marketing, or business development (BD) goals.

IDEA

When changing your site from one web address (or page) to another, it's important to include a "301 redirect." This is a piece of code on the website that tells the server that a page has moved to a new address. Say you updated an old "About Us" page and renamed it "Meet the Team." You want to make sure that if someone were to search for you and find the old "About Us" page on Google, that that link will send them to the new "Meet the Team" page.

Different firms use their websites in different ways, so what's most important to one firm might not be your priority. Define your website needs and capabilities (e.g., recruiting components, file sharing, partnering, integration with social media, video, etc.) based on the objectives that you've identified. For example, if you want subcontractors to be able to get to your bid list quickly to see what projects you're chasing, that's something that should be linked to on the main page. If you want to establish yourself as a thought leader, you may want to include a feed of your most recent (and frequently updated) tweets and blog posts.

Think about what technical requirements your firm might want for the next couple of years. If you love the idea of having videos on your page, but haven't actually shot a video yet, make sure that your website has a platform that's going to allow you to incorporate video in another year or two.

Another thing to consider is the ROI. A website is a huge investment for a firm, and it's important to be realistic about what you can really spend on its development. A Squarespace account—which is fairly basic, but lets you throw up some logos, photos, and add some content—is totally fine if that's all your budget allows for. The next step up would be WordPress—they provide both templates and customizable sites. The most-expensive option is to hire someone to build completely customized content management systems from the ground up.

It is worth noting, however, that these two examples (Squarespace and WordPress) are only two of the many options for website platforms currently available, and also that they may someday become obsolete. It's up to you to stay up-to-date on website platforms, as with all other forms of quickly-evolving technologies.

If you hire a consultant to help you with this, remember that the more upfront and open you are about your budget and ROI goals, the better. If your goal is to make another $2 million in new business from a certain service line, tell them. Here are some other examples of objectives that would help either you or a consultant to visualize the needs and organization of your site:

- Growing your email list by 20 percent
- Increase your number of Twitter followers
- More white papers downloaded
- An increased number of job seekers applying online

Knowing what success looks like before you start will help you to determine later whether you've achieved your objectives.

Responsive design is one of the biggest changes to website needs in the past few years. Even if you're not familiar with responsive design, you most likely rely on responsive websites every day. Responsive sites allow page layout, content, navigation, and other features to adjust, scale, and move based on the visitor's device. Firms leveraging responsive design can deliver an optimized experience to every visitor, regardless of how they access a website. Whether the display is on a smartphone, tablet, laptop, etc., a responsive site will accommodate it.

2.3.3 Integration

"Integration" is a sticky word—saying that you want your website to be integrated with social media or third parties is such a general statement that it doesn't really mean anything. It's important for your firm to define more specifically what integration means to them, either by crafting a clear outline of what elements of social media that you want to include, and where, or by finding examples of websites that integrate other media in a way that you really love. Do you want videos on your page? Should all of your most recent tweets show up on the home screen? Is it important to have "share" buttons on all of your articles? Whatever it is that you want, make sure that your developer and your team are speaking the same language. What does "integration" look like to you?

Incorporating social media into your firm's website is certainly vital to stay relevant in today's heavily connected world, and we'll talk more about developing a social media plan later in this section.

2.3.3.1 Search Engine Optimization (SEO)

Search engine optimization (SEO) is the process of improving the visibility of a website or a web page in search engines via natural (unpaid) search results. It's how you go about making a certain page or website rank "higher" when a specific term is entered into a search engine, such as Google. If a link to your site does not appear in the results on page one, it's unlikely that anyone will see it. The question is: How do you make your website more optimized? In other words, what changes can you make to your page to make search engines bring it up faster?

An SEO campaign involves the application of a relatively simple set of steps:

1. Keyword research
2. Content development
3. Web programming
4. Link building

Conducting keyword research is a good first step—every decision that you make thereafter is based on using the right words. You need to know what keywords and phrases people actually use to find products and services. The Google Keyword Tool, listed in the Related Resources section, is a good way to find commonly searched-for words and phrases. Doing this research first gives you the information that you need in order to create targeted content without resorting to guesswork.

TARGET POINT
Beware: Using too many keywords—a practice known as "keyword stuffing"—can hurt your search engine rankings. When choosing a keyword, think about the context in which a visitor will use it.

Once you know the language that people use to search for content, organize your website to conform to these findings. It is essential that a page contain both quality content and identified keywords, presented in an easy-to-navigate and appealing format; the way this information is structured and displayed will affect your rankings as well.

Creating descriptive categories and file names for the documents on your website will help keep your site organized and lead to better crawling of your documents by search engines. Make sure that the URLs are search-engine friendly by keeping the names short and including clear keywords. For example:

Better: www.mysite.com/services/construction-management

Worse: www.mysite.com/services/folder2/folder3/constructionmgmt-services.htm

If you understand nothing else about SEO, the most important lesson is consistency. A page on your site with a keyword found in the page name, the title, the headline, and the content, is far more likely to rank for that term than a page that doesn't leverage consistency.

Think like your clients. Text should be written using terminology common to the clients who procure your type of services. For example, industrial owners use the word "rigging" more often than equipment installation. In such cases, try to include both phrases in your content. However, never write website articles or sections purely to appeal to SEO. Your content must be unique, not just stuffed with keywords.

Search engines are smart and can easily identify duplicate (or very similar) content on a site's pages. Google defines duplicate content as "substantive blocks of content within or across domains that either completely match other content or are appreciably similar." If your site's content appears to be using deceptive keywords to manipulate search engine results, your site will be removed from the results altogether.

But while content is king, flawed programming can easily dethrone it. In terms of SEO, focus on text-based site development (wherever possible), a clean and logical site structure, and proper markup of key page elements. Search engines use computer programs called "web crawlers" (or "spiders") that browse the Internet in a methodical, automated manner to index website content. To be listed in the search engines, your content must be in HTML text format. Despite advances in crawling technology, search engines still have difficulty reading text that's contained in an image, video, or Flash file. Usage of rich media, such as Flash, should be considered enhancement to your content rather than a way to present original content. Such elements should be built on top of a solid content foundation that allows the site to function and still be usable without that media.

Your site's structure determines whether a search engine understands what the topic of your site is and how easily it will find and index content. The hierarchy of your site needs to follow a crawlable link structure so that all of your pages can be found. Pages that don't have links to them or that are hidden cannot be found. Consider keeping your site structure shallow. Think of it this way: The more clicks that it takes for a visitor to get from your home page to the deepest page on your site, the lower that page's ranking will be with most search engines. Reduce the number of clicks to get higher page rankings.

Here are some other suggestions for organizing your site to take full advantage of crawler technology:

- Include your targeted keywords in folder and page names—crawlers look at the list of files and folders on your site, and if the crawler finds a popular keyword there, your pages are more likely to get indexed higher up
- Invalid markup can cause layout issues and impede the search engines' ability to read and index your content—along with proper HTML syntax, important elements are content headings, page titles, and page descriptions using a description meta tag
- Double check your site's readability (see the Related Resources section for a list of sites that allow you to check what elements of your content are visible and able to be indexed by search engines)

In terms of building links, go for quality over quantity. The worth and relevance of each link matters much more than the total number that lead to your page, so focus on receiving fewer, high-value links rather than many low-quality or irrelevant ones. Submit articles to popular industry publications to get further mileage from backlinks. Links from pages that are marked as "important" by Google's crawlers are given more weight, and can in turn increase the importance of other pages. Your best bet is therefore to get big, reputable sources linking back to your own page and talking about all of the cool things that you're doing.

This is why it's so important to develop fresh, popular content on your website—if you're creating content that people want to link to, then links to your website will generate naturally from excited users. Write a new post at least once per month, if not once per week, to encourage people to link back to your site. If you have a website in 2015 and you don't make any additions or edits to your content for six months, you're shooting your SEO in the foot.

IDEA
One great way to build links is to ask for them. Clients and partners will often link to your site's home page or to a specific, relevant page on your site if asked.

2.3.4 Benchmark Competitors' Websites

Run a competitive analysis to see how well other firms are doing in terms of particular search terms that you want to be found for. This is most applicable on a local or regional level. For example, if your firm operates within the greater Detroit area, that's where you will face the most competition in SEO rankings for search terms like "Detroit architecture" or "MEP engineers in Detroit." The good news is that with specific terms like these it's fairly easy to climb in the rankings because there are only a small set of companies competing for those phrases.

Another comparison that you should pay attention to is how similar your website's visuals and messages are to your competitors. If everyone emphasizes that their firm is innovative on their main page, how do you differentiate your firm from the rest? Look at your competitors' sites and cover up their logo. Does it look different than yours? If the layout is the exact same (e.g., logo on the top left, big picture in the middle, Twitter feed on the right, etc.) maybe it's time for you to update your design.

2.3.5 Monitor and Manage Analytics

The number one tool for monitoring and managing your web data is Google Analytics. This service provided by Google is extremely helpful in understanding and optimizing how people use your website. You can see how long visitors stay on your website, how many pages they click, what days of the week are most popular, what pages are visited the most, and even where your visitors are located down to the city. In short, it tells you how your website is performing compared to every other website out there.

However, like any good tool, what you get out of Google Analytics depends entirely on how you use it. Most people install Google Analytics and step away, never to look at it again. Make sure that there is someone in your firm who is given the responsibility for reporting on the data collected. For example, Josh Miles of MilesHerndon reveals that in his company, the principals receive an email report from the digital in-house director every Friday. This means that at the end of every week, Miles is up-to-date on the activities of their email subscribers, social media numbers, and organic search numbers, as well as the director's thoughts and feedback on this information. Having someone who is really paying attention to this data is key; constant monitoring is the only way to discover trends in web activity, and changes to these trends are what will let you know whether different components of your web strategy are working well or need to be tweaked.

One of the most helpful Google Analytics reports to look at, Miles says, is a comparison of your site's popular pages (based on number of views) against the pages that get the longest views. From an engagement point of view, it is important that the most popular pages are also being looked at for the longest—a page that has a high ranking in both of these measures would be given a high engagement score. Some pages, such as "Contacts," are not supposed to have a high engagement score. You want someone to be able to find your firm's phone number quickly and move on. But for pages like individual projects, blog posts, white papers, case studies, and other places where you'd expect a user to linger, a low engagement score could be a problem. If people are working to get to a particular blog post, for example, but don't stick around long enough to read it, the consequential low engagement score could suggest that the content is boring, or doesn't give information on what the user was expecting to find.

The good thing about the Internet is that your website never goes to print—you never lose the ability to go back and edit those pages that aren't working. Adding key phrases, linking internally to your site, editing content, and cultivating the visual design of your site are all ways to improve optimization for search terms and get more people interacting with your website. And if the analytics reveal that a change that you made didn't get the results you wanted, you can always try, try again!

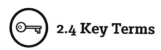 ## 2.4 Key Terms

Below are the main terms covered in this section:
- Communications plan
- Communications objectives
- Demographic characteristics
- Psychographic characteristics
- Social media
- Social media plan
- Inbound marketing
- Outbound marketing
- Content calendar
- 301 redirect
- Responsive design
- Integration
- Search engine optimization (SEO)
- Keyword
- Web crawlers
- Analytics
- Google Analytics

3 Media Relations

Success in media relations requires two things: (1) a strategic, targeted strategy, and (2) a compelling story to tell.

Applying these two elements and working successfully with the media are essential skills for marketing and communications professionals. Knowing the strategy and tactics of effective media relations—and using them at the right time, for the right reasons—will provide a competitive advantage in placing your firm's story in front of clients and key influencers.

By the end of this section, you should understand the following key points, and be able to use them in your promotional activity work:

- How to identify the online and print publications that are most important in your target markets
- How to customize media pitches to align with individual journalists, broadcasters, bloggers, and news outlets
- How to handle company communications in times of crisis and controversy
- Training firm leaders and spokespersons to work with the media

3.1 Strategy and Planning

PR strategy begins with the objectives established in the firm's communications plan. The communications plan should provide a differentiation message—what knowledge or expertise the company is sought for, and why clients repeatedly hire you (see section 2 for more information about developing a communications plan). This plan also identifies the targeted market sectors where PR can advance visibility, support BD, and build a long-term reputation by publishing the firm's work, expertise, and ideas.

Armed with the message and a specific audience sector, the process of building and maintaining a media presence is guided by a sound strategy. Ask your team, "Where are we looking to grow revenue in the next 12 to 24 months?"

Look for your firm's energetic, articulate leaders in these growth sectors. Are they willing to invest some time in sharing their expertise within a planned and targeted media outreach program? A willing collaborator, with the commitment to work with you, will make a huge difference in the quality and results of the effort.

3.2 Maintain a Media List

3.2.1 Research National Publications in Key Market Segments

The first step in creating a press list is researching which publications, blogs, and online forums cover the niche market sectors where you are seeking clients and influence. A/E/C publications should also be on the list. Researching targets for media outreach is easier than ever, thanks to the availability of online resources and media directories. The four outcomes of this research are to:

1. Build a media list of target reporters, editors, broadcasters and bloggers; and update this list regularly

2. Find and review editorial calendars to determine when a target media organization may be covering your topic, clients, region or expertise

3. Learn the editorial mission, reader focus, subscriber demographics and specific journalist beats within the target media outlets

4. Utilize LinkedIn, Twitter, Instagram and other social channels to learn about the interests, past writing and current activities of the editors and writers you may want to approach with news, a pitch or a contributed article

The most frequent complaint by journalists about marketing and PR people is that they don't have a clue about how or where a story may (or may not) fit into the publication. These journalists say that marketers rarely bother to learn about their editorial mission and readership prior to calling or emailing. Failing to do this basic homework is a surefire way to alienate journalists and derail your story. Take the time to learn how to fit your pitch into the unique needs of the target publication, broadcast outlet or blog.

For example, the editorial mission of Building Design and Construction (BD&C) magazine is to cover the entire building team: owner, architect, engineer, builder, etc. An effective pitch to BD&C editors addresses how the proposed topic, project or news story is relevant to the team dynamic. How does the achievement or idea benefit team collaboration or add knowledge or value to the collaborative process of design and construction?

With any target publication, your research needs to reveal whether a particular target publishes news release information, whether they accept contributed articles, how long their lead times are, etc. Of equal importance is to learn who among the editors, reporters and broadcasters covers the particular beat you are pitching.

Where can you find all of this information? The starting point is the "About Us" and "Advertise" sections on the website of the target newspaper, magazine, broadcast station or online publication. This should provide basic information on the staff, editorial mission, editorial calendar and reader demographics.

More thorough contact information can be found in commercial media directories, a reference staple of all PR professionals. A list of the most popular media directories is included in the Related Resources section. If your budget doesn't have room for purchasing a subscription for these directories, check your city library to see if they have an online subscription you can use.

Next, validate your research by finding out what your clients read, both online and in print. Each market sector offers several trade and professional journals, association newsletters, online and print magazines, blogs and newsfeeds. Ask your clients, and your in-house client ambassadors, which outlets are most read and respected.

Lastly and most importantly, read the publications. Get to know their unique purpose and focus. Look for special sections or recurring features where your story may fit. If you cannot access a copy online, call the publication and ask for a media kit, which will contain a sample issue or two and information about reader demographics.

Search the publication's archives by topic to see which reporter or editor you need to know. Understand in advance the publication's criteria for articles, author submissions and methods of contact. Each has its own philosophy for considering stories, and many have different slots within the publication where you can aim: guest editorials, case studies, news sections and feature pages. One size never fits all.

In an interview conducted by Michael Reilly, FSMPS, for the SMPS *Marketer*, *Metropolis Magazine* editor-in-chief Susan Szenasy said that her team "looks for more than just a nice design or an interesting case study. It's important that a story has a cultural or an environmental connection….a system or solution that takes a project in a direction that needs to be taken to better serve the owner."

This is an important insight for anyone approaching *Metropolis* with a story on a recent innovative solution. By reading the publication and becoming familiar with their reporting and point of view, you learn about the editorial slant and subtleties. Armed with this insight, you are ready to build a relationship.

3.2.2 Local List

In addition to building a national media list of target market sector publications and A/E/C editors, writers and bloggers, a comprehensive local/regional list is important as well. Integrate local business publications, news outlets and online/social media sites into your list using the methods outlined above. These publications may be general business news outlets, such as the weekly business journals in most cities, and many will cover commercial real estate, design and construction as part of their editorial mission. Some work from an editorial calendar. Identifying opportunities to share knowledge, send news or write an opinion piece is a great way to tap into a special interest community and gain regional recognition for your firm.

3.3 Draft News Releases

The venerable news release continues to be the most commonly used (and frequently misused) media relations tool. The purpose of a news release is to succinctly compose your news story and use the release to inform editors of its facts and news appeal.

A few guidelines for preparing news releases:
- **Include news.** It sounds trite, but many news releases never survive past the first look by your recipient. Identify what the news item is—a new application of technology, a project milestone, a first-ever use of a construction technique or a new service developed in response to a significant shift in market demand.
- **Make it interesting.** A release on a completed project, a company anniversary or an office opening will be of great interest to those inside your company. To

those outside and with the press, the appeal is close to zero. Take the initiative to look for something newsworthy or distinctive. Is the company celebrating the anniversary by increasing support to local nonprofits, hosting a competition for young engineers or creating a scholarship named for the firm's founder? What's driving the need for a new office in another city? How did your recent project move the dial on new technology, sustainability, creative design or project management?

- **Keep it brief.** The ideal length of a news release is 400 to 500 words. Use a companion fact sheet for all of the extras, such as the list of project partners. Include a short quote and key facts, but be economical. Once you're ready to draft a news release, follow universally accepted formats. A release answers the who, what, where, when, why and how within an inverted pyramid with the most important information at the top. This makes it easy for editors to assess the key facts and to cut and paste from the top to match the space they have to fill.

- **Include an image.** Most online news pages and printed news sections feature an image with a short amount of text. Some of these pages prominently display the photo to catch the reader's eye, and show only the first sentence or two of the text up front. Readers must click through to read the whole entry. Without a photo, the risk is high that your news will never make the cut.

- **Use quotes.** Include a quote from the firm's representative—either the CEO or a designated spokesperson—and write it using colloquial language that sounds like something a person would say during a conversation with the reader. Client quotes are helpful to include, and it's not unusual for the client to ask the person seeking the quote to draft something for them to review and approve. This presents a great opportunity to showcase what makes the project interesting and how your team provided an exceptional solution, service or team.

One important use for the full release is your own website, which should have a news section, if not an entire designated "news room." Besides news, the designated section provides essential information on the firm, both black-and-white and color photographs, bios of key people and links within the site for further information. At the same time that you distribute your release, you'll want to upload the same document to your site, as well as related background materials.

 TARGET POINT
SEO of News Releases
Over the past few years, much of the focus of news release writing was on how well the release could be engineered to secure favorable search rankings. Techniques used to accomplish this goal include peppering multiple hyperlinks throughout the release, or using keywords that would be favored by Google's search algorithms.
The difficulty with trying to create favorable rankings for news releases is that Google

continuously changes the protocol for how documents such as news releases are ranked. To prevent the intentional engineering of search rankings, Google has, in the past 18 months, introduced a series of adjustments to its algorithms and protocols directed specifically at news releases.

The lesson for marketing and PR professionals is to focus on the news release and its intended audience: the media. Provide what they need, make it clear and include essential data. If you want to check on the current treatment of news releases for SEO outcomes, you can search the topic and learn the latest protocols.

3.3.1 Sample News Releases

A news release should be written on official letterhead. Below is a sample of a news release:

News Release: August 20, 2015
Contact: Jaime Flores at 800.292.7677 Ext. 228 or jaime@smps.org

SMPS *Marketer* Magazine Wins Awards for Redesign

Alexandria, VA—The Society for Marketing Professional Services (SMPS), the premier A/E/C marketing and business development association, is pleased to announce it has won a 2015 Hermes Creative Award for its *Marketer* publication. SMPS entered *Marketer* as a magazine redesign and was awarded Platinum, the highest honor. *Marketer* also earned Bronze in the EXCEL Awards competition.

Marketer was completely redesigned and made its debut in October 2014. The Society partnered with TGD Communications, a full-service agency located in Alexandria, VA, to revamp the publication. *Marketer* gained a contemporary look and included a new emphasis on editorial to match the associations' educational focus.

Hermes Creative Awards recognizes outstanding work in the industry while promoting the philanthropic nature of marketing and communications professionals. More than 6,000 entries were received and approximately 15% of these entries were Platinum-level winners.

The EXCEL Awards, organized by the Association Media & Publishing, is the largest and most prestigious award program that recognizes excellence in leadership in nonprofit association media, publishing, marketing, and communications. Only 25% of the associations who entered the competition won an award.

Jaime Flores, SMPS Vice President of Marketing and Communications, says, "*Marketer* being recognized with these awards speaks volumes about the hard work done by our staff, content contributors, editorial board, and TGD to produce a publication worthy of our membership. Because of the contributions of these talented folks, *Marketer* serves as the leading journal for the A/E/C marketing and business development community."

For more information about SMPS or *Marketer*, please contact: JH Flores at 703.549.6117, x228.

###

About the Society for Marketing Professional Services

The Society for Marketing Professional Services (SMPS) is the only marketing association offering A/E/C professionals the etwork, knowledge, and training to build business. SMPS offers members professional development, leadership opportunities, and marketing resources to advance their careers. SMPS represents a dynamic network of 6,300+ marketing and business development professionals from architectural, engineering, planning, interior design, construction, and specialty consulting firms. The Society and its chapters benefit from the support of 3,650 design and building firms, encompassing 80% of the Engineering News-Record Top 500 Design Firms and Top 400 Contractors.

SMPS Headquarters, 123 N. Pitt Street, Suite 400, Alexandria, VA 22314
PH: 800.292.7677 • WB: smps.org • EM: info@smps.org

3.3.2 Assign Responsibility to In-House Staff or an Outside Consultant

Many firms have someone in-house who is responsible for PR, while others prefer to use an outside person or agency. In-house people are not always trained or experienced in media relations, which makes it harder for them to create effective publicity or even explain to their companies what will work or not, and why. Their time is often prioritized to proposals and other sales-specific activities, and as a consequence, PR suffers. The advantage of in-house PR is that the marketing staff knows what's going on and has access to insights and information that a consultant may not. Still, experienced consultants know what to look for and what dots to connect.

A combined effort that taps the knowledge and access of the in-house pros with the honed skills and media relations expertise of the outside consultant works well for many firms.

There are several types of firms involved with marketing communications that you might turn to for outside help:

- **Advertising agencies.** They write, design and place advertisements and advise firms on options for advertising spending, including digital and social channel buys.
- **PR firms.** They advise firms on message strategy and how to reach key audiences. They plan, write and execute campaigns which may include producing content for media distribution/placement and for publishing within a firm's own channels (e.g., website, blog, video and other social and digital domains).
- **Specialists.** These include web developers, graphic designers, copywriters, SEO firms, content creators, videographers, etc.

See section 11 for more on the process of choosing and hiring outside consultants.

3.4 Distribute Approved Release

Once you have a news release written and have the necessary client approval, you can move on to media outreach and distribution. Depending on the type of release, there are two options for distribution.

1. **Send it out yourself.** Use your in-house media list to send the release to each recipient one by one. This has the advantage of being more personal, as you can customize the greeting and message to each individual addressee.

2. **Use a wire distribution service.** Broadcasting your news releases via a wire service such as BusinessWire or PR Newswire gives you access to all of the connections that the service has. The advantage of this is a potentially wider distribution. Even so, there's no guarantee that the release will reach the right person who covers your field, and it may be viewed as generic by those who do see it.

The way that you decide to distribute your news releases will depend on your firm's circumstances. Publicly owned companies regulated by the FCC (Federal Communications Commission) are required to release news to every outlet at the same time, so as to avoid creating an advantage for one particular recipient or consumer audience over another. In that case, a wire distribution service is the best option to ensure that every recipient gets it at the exact same moment.

Wire services charge for annual membership and sell "circuits" for your story, so your information goes right into the newsroom of the publications that you want to reach and remains in the service's archive long after the initial distribution. Most often, PR firms or marketing departments are the subscribers.

3.5   Contacting the Media

Whether following up on your news release or pitching a feature article, there are important considerations that are part of building a positive relationship with individuals making their living on the media side.

Relationships dictate success in business, and media relations is no exception. You must cultivate a relationship with editors, reporters and bloggers whose interest you are seeking for your stories, firm and clients. Focus on what will help them by taking the time to learn about them as individuals. What do they cover: breaking news, trends, CEOs? How can your knowledge, projects, clients and stories fit with his or her approach and writing?

One editor summed this principle up best: "Get to know us. We receive a tremendous volume of unsolicited material, so we naturally pay more attention to those whose work we know and respect."

Your job as a marketing or PR professional is to be a resource and educator for the journalists who cover the A/E/C industry and those of your clients. Be helpful, respect the incredible demands on their time, and remember that you are after a relationship that will endure over many years.

To create and sustain these relationships, here are some actions and advice:

- **Pass along story ideas and interesting information to your media partners that are not related to your firm or your pitch.**
- **Share their stories with your network via Twitter, LinkedIn, Facebook, Instagram and other social channels.** Their employers closely watch the digital footprint of stories published, since traffic back to the source of the story is a key metric for advertisers and publishers.
- **Offer to provide client input, quotes or images for stories that you see coming up on the editorial calendar.** You don't always need a full-blown (or overblown) pitch to be the star of their next feature.
- **When you pitch a trend story, provide examples and sources beyond your firm, including competitors if you know that there is something worthwhile**

to pass along. Journalists need more than one company's experience to tell the story of a trend.

- **Respect the inbox of media pros.** Contact them only when you are certain that your pitch, news release or byline idea is appropriate to his or her responsibility and beat. Never spam them with shotgun-style releases or non-personalized "Dear Editor" pitches. Be human and personal.

3.5.1 Follow-Up Protocols

One of the most frequently asked questions in media relations is, "How do I follow up on pitches and news releases?" Each situation and relationship is different, but here are some basic actions to take, based on advice from numerous journalists:

- **Never call an editor to ask, "Did you get my news release?"** If it didn't bounce back to you, they got it. If you call, make sure that you have something new to offer.
- **Don't assume that being an advertiser provides an advantage in gaining coverage.** Legitimate journalists pay little attention to who is or is not buying advertising. Most will be put off if you suggest that they should.
- **A brief email or phone called placed two to three weeks after sending an article idea is appropriate.** They could easily have overlooked the original message. Don't assume that there is no interest when you haven't heard back.
- **When something is published, send a short thank-you note.** A handwritten note sent to an editor or reporter following a successful collaboration will be remembered.

3.6 Publish Newsletter or Journal Articles

Publishing articles is one of the most accessible tools for thought-leading firms wanting to demonstrate their expertise. This tool involves writing informative, helpful articles to be published in magazines read by the target audience. This can include third-party newsletters as well as the fast-growing realm of electronic media. Some of these are the online-only content of traditional print magazines, third-party blogs and websites, and web-only publications. It means something longer than a typical blog entry, but shorter than a book—most expert-written articles in print magazines are somewhere between 500 and 2,000 words. It's enough for you to show your firm's expertise, through work that takes a few hours to do.

Any tool has its strengths and weaknesses, and it's important to understand the relevant factors for article writing. One of the biggest strengths is reliability. If you follow the guidelines here, you can be reasonably certain that your efforts will bear fruit. Also, because most trade and professional publications are focused on a narrow readership, it's a good way to target your message to the specific markets that you want to reach.

On the other hand, it's a slow burn. Trade magazines range from weekly publications to quarterlies (publishing four times a year). Because most magazines are put together by just a handful of people, the work goes on well in advance—your message may take two or three months to appear. Some business publications don't accept articles from experts, as theirs are written mostly by staff members or professional freelance writers. They may only take opinion articles from high-profile individuals. In general, any magazine over about 80,000 circulation is unlikely to take expert-written articles. This includes most magazines distributed on newsstands. The best way to find out if the magazine you're considering accepts contributed articles is to read through it and see if there are any.

3.6.1 Choose a Topic

All business magazines focus their coverage and markets, and the editor is highly motivated to publish articles of interest to that designated audience. She or he will want to cover topics that the reader will find nowhere else and to omit those that aren't specifically targeted to that audience. Align your article topics to the client world—the problems, trends and needs that you've discovered through the research and planning contained in your marketing and communications plan.

To select the right magazine for your purpose, you need to understand that business magazines usually segment themselves in one of three ways: by industry, profession or occupation, or geography. Shopping Center World, for example, is targeted toward the retail commercial real-estate industry. It discusses design and construction, leasing, property management, and other topics of interest to people in this industry. Its readers are interested in many different topics, provided that there's a clear link to their field. They want to know about architecture, for example, but only as it relates to shopping malls. They won't be interested in the architecture of hotels, schools or other buildings unless there are some clear lessons to be applied to shopping centers. The same goes for legal issues. The editor wants to know about the law as it pertains to topics such as trespassing in these quasi-public spaces, about landlord-tenant law for retailers and about making common area fee agreements acceptable to retail tenants. Don't bother to present the editor with ideas that don't have a direct connection with that magazine's readers.

Some publications are targeted to a specific profession or occupation. If you want to reach chief financial officers (CFOs) with the message that your firm's ideas can save money, for example, look for publications that reach this community. As with industry publications, editors of these magazines want to provide coverage that is exclusive to their subscriber's interests. A magazine for CFOs might also be interested in an article on architecture, provided it's specifically about how employees can be more satisfied and productive within certain kinds of work environments. However, the editor will be interested in other financial topics as well, so if you can address these issues, this may be worth pursuing.

Geography-oriented business magazines demand a heavy local angle to their coverage. If you want coverage in such a magazine, it helps to be locally based or at least to have a local office. Magazines like this are interested in local organizations

and local issues. If your firm contains consultants on retail strategy, for example, you might write about the retail sector trends in the geographic market you want to reach. Experience has found that geographic-based publications tend to be mostly written by journalists and many are not particularly open to outside contributions. Some may accept a regular column, for example, by a local lawyer or accountant.

> **TARGET POINT**
> Increase your article's credibility by backing up the statements that you make with research. If, for example, you were writing about the best way to design a classroom, you could cite research about how learning is more successful in a classroom that has daylight. Citing a study that shows how successful daylighting is in 12 schools turns your article from an opinion piece into a source of credible information.

3.6.2 Getting Published

Many professionals seeking to get their names into print will spend evenings and weekends crafting an article and then sending it to an editor, only to get a form rejection note in return, or no response at all. It's demoralizing and can cause firms to avoid article writing as a marketing tool.

To understand why an article might be rejected, consider the publishing process from the editor's point of view. They likely have a very specific task—to inform readers about a targeted topic. This person will therefore be wary of articles that don't address this topic or perspective. Many article ideas received are wide off of the mark or are unusable product pitches. He or she is busy due to a daunting daily flood of news releases, backgrounders, newsletters and other mail.

The editor's task includes deciding on issue themes, determining which topics will match those themes and then putting it all together. This includes copy editing, layout, commissioning photographs, creating other graphics and production. As well as producing the magazine, they may be required to maintain a regular blog, an active presence on Twitter and help organize one or two conferences per year. Therefore, most editors simply don't have time for articles or article ideas that don't meet their editorial mandate.

Here are some ways to increase the chances that the ideas that you present will be acceptable to the editor:

- **Become familiar with the magazine.** Many editors complain that they get plenty of article ideas that sound like interesting stories, but not stories that are right for them. Often this is because the person proposing the idea did not take the time to become familiar with the magazine's mandate and target market. To avoid the error of presenting the wrong idea to the wrong publication, your first step should be to go back to your research on publications to find out what issues and themes will be of interest to this particular publication.

- **Fit into the editorial calendar.** Most publications have an editorial calendar that sets the schedule for the theme of each issue. It is usually under "Advertising" or "Media Kit" on the publication's website. The editor will be looking for articles on these topics. Sometimes, your article will have a seasonal factor. If you're proposing an idea on how to make sure that the summer road construction season inconveniences drivers as little as possible, suggest this for a summer issue. The media directories listed in the Related Resources section have a searchable online database of editorial calendars where one can search by topic, region or type of publication.

Once you have completed the steps above, you're ready to approach the editor. The best way to do this is not through a completed article. Many editors don't want to take the time to read unsolicited manuscripts, which are articles that they haven't asked for. Instead, they prefer to receive a query letter, which is a mini-proposal for the article. This way, they can evaluate the ideas in less than one minute, rather than having to wade through an entire manuscript to find out if it contains anything that they can use. A good query letter contains four parts:

1. **What's your story idea?** In one or two sentences, say that you want to write a "contributed article" for the magazine and what your topic is.

2. **Why would readers of this particular magazine be interested?** All editors want content that is specific to their readership; and even if it seems obvious to you, it's important to show the editor that your topic fits the editorial purpose.

3. **What are the points that you will cover?** In three or four bullet points of one line each, indicate what you plan to talk about. This helps to reassure the editor that you've thought through your topic.

4. **Can the readers trust what you write?** Indicate why you're qualified to discuss the topic—your academic and professional qualifications and your experience in the industry, in two or three sentences. The editor wants to make sure that readers will be getting sound information.

3.6.3 Determine the Communication Channel

There are many different communication channels—blog posts, white papers, print magazines, online magazines and paid advertorials all have their place—and you must choose between them based on the style of article that you want to write and your target audience. We've covered print magazines extensively above, so this section will talk briefly about your other options: blog posts, white papers, online magazines and paid advertorials.

Which is the right medium for you? It depends on several factors. One is whether the proposed topic can be reasonably dealt with in the space of the medium. A typical white paper is 12 pages long, for instance. It could be that the best medium is a series of articles in a business magazine or a blog that lays out the topic over several installments. Or, the best solution could be a video in which the author is able to demonstrate her or his personality, along with some charts and graphs, with site photographs.

It's also important to determine your purpose in writing. Is it just to demonstrate thought leadership on an issue, as a way of positioning the firm as a preferred source of solutions? Is it to demonstrate the benefits of a new technology that the firm has acquired, in hopes of using that technology on the reader's behalf? Is it to introduce a new member of the firm to potential clients?

The third point to think through is the characteristics of the reader—how will they want to engage with the material? Different audiences gravitate towards different mediums, and you should know where to find yours. Using social media—both third-party profiles and your firm's own—to cross-promote content and provide links for easy access to content is a good way to ensure that more viewers will see an article no matter where it appears.

> **IDEA**
> Extend the reach and value of the topic by selecting multiple channels and repurposing the length and format to match the channel.

3.6.3.1 Blog Posts

Your blog offers an opportunity to share short articles with your audiences and to engage with them by taking comments. Like other tactics described in this section, the most effective blogs don't just blast out company news and announcements; they help audiences and offer points of view. Here are some ways to make your blog post as effective as possible:

- **Make the post brief and on-point.** If posts get too long, consider breaking them up (this will also help you to fill out your content calendar, which is discussed further in section 4).
- **Link to other online sources, when applicable.**
- **Use social media or email to drive traffic to your blog.**
- **With the opportunity for engagement through comments comes a responsibility to respond.** Understand that not all comments on your blog post will be positive, and address comments promptly.

In the event that you receive negative comments on your post, keep calm. Although you want to be prompt in your response, you must also take the time to think before you write back. It's natural to become defensive, but you do not want your response to be negatively colored by this feeling. Use phrases such as "I understand," "Thank you for responding to my post," and "I'm happy to discuss this with you." Then, you may want to take the discussion offline to address the specific concern.

TARGET POINT
The Perfect Post

Wessler Engineering, a civil and environmental engineering firm, launched its blog soon after redoing its website. With the use of inbound marketing software to support and measure its efforts, Wessler maintains a weekly blog that is promoted through email and social media platforms.

Through questionnaires and brainstorming with staff, the firm discovers what topics are relevant to its target audience. Wessler makes sure that its posts are related to these topics, and often includes links to videos and downloadable case studies to beef up the content.

As a sign of its success, Wessler won nine projects after writing a blog post titled: "Uh Oh, I Received a Letter from IDEM (Indiana Department of Environmental Management)."

Key Concepts for this Story:
- It is important to take the time to learn what topics are of interest for your target audience
- Blogs can be an important part of an integrated communications network
- Blog posts that are relevant and timely for a target audience can be instrumental in generating new work

3.6.3.2 White Papers

A longstanding tool for demonstrating thought leadership, in some cases, white papers have descended into undisguised product pitches, particularly in high-technology fields. As a result, their reputation has been tarnished for some readers. But it seems that a new wave of white papers, based on the principles of content marketing, is bringing this medium back to respectability. This wave is based not so much on the theme of, "Here's what we want to tell you about us," but of, "Here is some unbiased information that will help you to solve a problem." It doesn't look so much at the solutions that your firm offers, as it does the client problems that it solves.

Given the flexibility and ease of use found in current page design, there is really no excuse for a white paper that is just a solid mass of text. Break it up using subheadings, bulleted lists, diagrams, graphs and charts, and photographs. A qualified designer, on staff or external, can punch a just-the-text document into something that meets current expectations of professionalism.

Who writes it? The named author could—if this person is an efficient writer and won't take a week of time that could have been billed, and is able to explain the topic in reader friendly terms. It may be better to have the paper ghostwritten, either by a member of the marketing staff or an external freelancer. Possibly, the named author does a first draft, which is then rewritten by a skilled writer and passed back to the author for review and correction as needed.

As with any kind of writing, often the first sentence is the most critical—grab the reader's attention right away with some useful information or a thought-provoking question, or you risk losing the person's attention. If the paper is making a recommendation about a possible solution, it is important to clearly address the problem and establish that it needs to be solved. After writing the paper, ask yourself—if I were a potential client, would I be persuaded of the need to take action by what is in the paper?

3.6.3.3 Online Magazines

Over the years, magazine websites have evolved into a place for editors to put the constant stream of news releases, for which there is no room for in the print publication, as well as contributed articles that don't fit in the magazine pages. Add blogs, Twitter feeds, videos, slide shows and other information that, the editors hope, creates a must-read online community for people in the magazine's target market. This means that expert contributors may find that their articles, which they hope to be printed in the pages of the dead-tree magazine, are diverted online. However, it also means that there are more opportunities available—publications that rarely or never accept outside contributions in print may take them for their online edition.

Online articles are different from print articles. They're generally shorter, punchier, with more subheadings and more bullet points. They also allow the opportunity to include links to videos, podcasts and other electronic content. As of this writing, tablet-based magazines are being touted as a wave of the future. So far, these provide mostly just the text of the articles displayed online. Few trade magazines have progressed as far as the larger publications have in terms of having electronic content to go along with the articles. This is changing, and firms able to provide value-added content will find a warm welcome from editors interested in providing more than text and pictures.

3.6.3.4 Paid Advertorials

An advertorial as defined by Merriam-Webster as "an advertisement that imitates editorial format." Most readers can readily identify the advertorial and many will simply skip over this page. However, if an advertorial is an option that you wish to explore, there are a few things to keep in mind:

- Make sure that your piece is in line with the content and feel of the publication
- Keep your advertising elements (such as a logo) minimal, so that it truly feels like a part of the publication
- Understand the readers of the publication and write to what they need and want to know

3.7 Train Staff to Interact with Media

3.7.1 Identify Personnel to Interact With the Press

The person chosen to interact with the press is an entirely situational decision, based on who can most credibly and articulately present the relevant information. In some cases—a big, positive announcement such as a merger, acquisition or huge new project—the CEO is the best person for the job. However, if there's been a controversial event, it's usually best not to put the CEO onto the media's front line. Negative publicity, such as a death at a construction site or the arrest of a key person in the firm, is best handled by a spokesperson.

In most cases, that spokesperson should be a member of the firm, usually the marketing director or principal. In other cases, it could be a regional office leader, sector leader, or a project executive with knowledge of the topic or project in discussion. In all of these scenarios, individuals need to be trained to comfortably handle the often unpredictable role of talking with the press.

Section 11 will discuss crisis communication in greater depth.

3.7.2 Training

Building the skills needed to be an effective spokesperson can be taught, rehearsed and perfected. This is not a skill taught in school, nor learned on the way up through the ranks. Training spokespersons and leadership in media conversations can be accomplished with a formal program by an outside expert, or handled in-house by an experienced media relations and marketing professional. If you use an outside trainer, it is beneficial to select someone who understands the A/E/C business and is familiar with the dynamic of client relationships and the risks inherent to the business. The most effective types of training will incorporate real-world situations drawn from A/E/C examples that give your staff practice communicating both positive and negative information, and responding to issues that arise with clients, their decisions and their projects.

Few design and construction professionals are natural public speakers or interview subjects, much as they might welcome the one-on-one. Ideally, there is someone in your firm who can give the big picture as well as the details and answer questions easily, not defensively—even though it's their job to get the marketing message across, uncanned.

3.8 Key Terms

Below are the main terms covered in this section:

- Press list
- Editorial calendar
- News release
- Wire distribution service
- Advertorial

4   Create Digital Content

As brochures and other print materials lose their dominance in the business world, many other forms of messaging have risen to fill the need for corporate communication. Companies now have the means to create sophisticated audio and visual materials to get their targeted messages out via the Web.

By the end of this section, you should understand the following key points, and be able to use them in your promotional activity work:

- How videos can be a powerful and increasingly affordable way to influence a target market
- How to leverage podcasts and other web-based communications into an effective way for content users to absorb information

4.1   Using Multimedia

Ink on paper is diminishing in its influence as more people seek information from electronic media. A few points on making that transition:

- As in a good piece of print collateral, multimedia involves storytelling. Tell one that shows your company's skills through one of its projects. Because of the limitations of a video lasting only a few minutes, you can't tell the whole story, so be able to hone it down to the essentials.
- Decide what level of production quality that you want and then be sure that you have the resources to obtain that quality. It must be consistent with your message—an architecture firm that claims to deliver stellar design, for example, will need a high level of production in multimedia. High-level work will probably require a skilled outside source.
- An already-stretched marketing team might want to expand its multimedia offerings, but be prepared to let it drop some existing tasks—or put aside enough of your budget to outsource it, possibly with the understanding that the external supplier will help teach your staff to produce its own work.

4.2   Videos

Many A/E/C firms have the potential to provide great visuals—wind turbines that spin, water that splashes, cranes that move, cement trucks that roll…and a consulting archaeologist who can show the cannon balls that she pulled out of a river. But A/E/C firms have been slow to embrace this medium.

4.2.1   Video Marketing

The terms "viral video" and "viral video social media marketing" are used to describe videos that are shared at a rapid pace across multiple online and mobile platforms.

An entire industry has developed to focus on the swift promotion of videos to viewers across available online outlets such as Facebook, Twitter, blogs and LinkedIn. Video marketing has become a major part of any complete marketing campaign.

Through the use of video, firms are able to market and promote their brand platform in a manner that encourages interaction between their customers and potential clients. Through the simple task of "sharing" and forwarding video content, the viewer becomes an engaged participant in the marketing campaign. There are more than three billion active Internet users each year and studies have found that over 75 percent of those connected to the Internet watch at least one video per day on their PC or mobile device.

In a 2014 report titled Video Statistics: The Marketer's Summary, the technology firm Invodo stated that over 52 percent of the marketing professionals surveyed named video as the best content for producing a good ROI. Marketing professionals assert that the presence of video increases email open rates by 20 percent. As the impact of videos on marketing continues to grow, the importance of professionally designed videos will be vital when trying to reach diverse audiences.

The impact of video on SEO is another consideration. For a firm that is trying to position its brand in a seemingly crowded field, videos can offer a competitive advantage. Through an increase of shares and video views, and with the proper backend meta-tagging and online backlinks, marketers can increase their chances that search engines such as Google, Chrome and Firefox will pull their websites and content first when viewers and potential clients conduct an online search.

A well-produced video, along with a good linking strategy, can result in significant online rankings growth for a firm. But it is not just about creating relevant video content—the quality of that video's content and the delivery of the message within to your target audience also matters. How you produce your video can play a major role in whether or not it is shared or continuously viewed.

4.2.1.1 The Rise of Mobile Video Production

Due to their size and affordability, DSLRs/HDSLRs and small, hand-held HD camcorders are quickly becoming the go-to tools for mobile filmmaking. With camera manufacturers increasingly putting HD video recording tools in their digital cameras—including large sensors, quality performance in low light, manageable depth of field and the availability of different lens ranges—they are now an affordable option for producing quality video. When properly outfitted with a quality external audio device and a camera stabilizer mount such as a Steadicam, camera rig or stationary tripod, cameras have the potential to produce broadcast-quality video.

The ability to produce and edit high-quality video in-house, combined with the ability to deploy the videos in the body of an email (increasing the likelihood that customers and potential clients will engage with the content in the email), makes DSLRs and camcorders an important tool in the arsenal of any marketer.

4.2.1.2 DSLR vs HD camcorder

For "run and gun" short film, commercials and event video production, many filmmakers are using DSLRs properly fitted with mobile accessories. In many cases, DSLR cameras and HD 4K camcorders come equipped with a sensor that is 40 percent larger than the standard 35mm large video cameras used in Hollywood productions. By leveraging the robust capacity of DSLRs, filmmakers do not have to rely upon production crews and bulky, expensive accessories to create short videos. The results are beautiful, cinematic-quality videos at a fraction of the cost. The quality of DSLR films has proven reliable even for large-scale productions such as the Lord of the Rings trilogy. With a manageable budget and specific training, many A/E/C firms can shoot, store, and disseminate quality video.

Although many DSLR cameras are great for filmmaking, it is important to recognize their limitations. If you are seeking a fast, autofocus device for shooting video, an HD camcorder may be the better option. Only a few DSLRs have a quality autofocus feature that can rival their camcorder counterparts in terms of speed and ease of use. However, if you prefer using a DSLR camera due to its size and additional ability to shoot quality photos at high resolutions, a manually adjustable, follow-focus device can be purchased as an affordable accessory. The follow-focus device attaches to your DSLR and produces a near-cinematic quality depth of field (focus pull). In addition, attaching an external monitor to your DSLR camera creates a larger viewing screen area.

Aside from the ability to autofocus easily, HD camcorders also come equipped with audio and video output/input slots that are not often found on DSLRs. The superior XLR and HDMI inputs, a standard feature in many HD camcorders, are preferred for audio and video recording over the smaller 1/8-inch mini-jack and RCA cables that are standard on mobile devices. HD camcorders with these outputs/inputs offer the ability to access these features without purchasing additional accessories for a DSLR.

4.2.1.3 Frame Rates and Resolution

Most DSLR and HD Camcorders can record in a full 1080p HD resolution of 1920×1080 pixels. This is usually accomplished at the recommended USA cinema, Blu-ray standard of 24fps to 30fps (frames per second). The devices also offer the option to shoot at the lower 720p HD resolution of 1280×720 pixels. Although it is not Blu-ray standard, this is twice the resolution of the older DVD formats. Use of either the 1080p or 720p is recommended for video production because they are preferred by popular, video-sharing websites such as YouTube and Vimeo. There are higher formats: 2160p, known as 4K and consisting of 3840×2160 pixels; and 4320p, known as 8K and consisting of 7680×4320 pixels. Both of these formats can be shot at 50fps to 60fps, but, as of 2016, there are few digital outlets that broadcast at these resolutions.

The preferred format for viewing video and the recommended aspect ratio is 16:9 as widescreen. The 24fps is the recommended speed since it most closely mimics the perception of the human eye. The 4k frame rates can make objects appear too digital. For best results, it is recommended that all encoded audio be at a constant rate of 192

to 320 kbps. If your final product is too large to upload online due to the audio size, lowering the encoded audio less than 128 kbps is not recommended.

4.2.1.4 Recording Quality Audio

Recording quality audio is often overlooked, but it is a key component in video production. Although most DSLR and HD camcorders are equipped with built-in microphones, generally these standard features are not adequate for recording cinema-quality audio. One notable complication is the use of Automatic Gain Control (AGC). AGC is applied in devices to compensate for small microphones by raising the gain for ambient soft sounds. AGC can create a finished product with unbalanced audio, a clear "hiss" or "hum," or low/garbled audio.

Using built-in microphones can produce unpredictable audio outcomes. This can increase production costs and timeframes. The only way to correct these shortcomings is to utilize an external audio device. External audio devices attach to video recording devices in order to properly capture audio. The following external devices are used by video professionals to maximize sound during production:

- **Shotgun microphone.** A shotgun microphone is one of the main audio tools used by mobile cinematographers working with a single camera. The microphone resembles the barrel of a shotgun and it has the ability to capture its intended target when aimed directly. Their long, narrow pickup pattern can record audio at a distance while suppressing unwanted sounds from the sides of the microphone. These microphones work best when mounted on a boom pole or on a camera hot shoe that is placed a few feet away from the subject.

- **Lavalier.** Lavalier microphones, with their small size and ability to be placed inconspicuously on the subject, are your best option for capturing superior sound when recording people. They are highly portable, do not require additional personnel for operation, and record at an exceptionally high quality. These small microphones usually come with two pieces, the transmitter and the receiver. They can be either wired or wireless. Wireless devices rely upon matching frequencies.

- **Lavs are usually placed near the chest and throat area to capture the subject's voice.** The general rule is to place the lav about 10 inches from the subject's mouth and to adjust the live capture test audio levels within the receiver or camera before you begin recording. Since lavs are small and are placed close to the recording subject, they are sensitive to noise created by movement. Lavaliers are great for interviews, but they do not offer the smooth sound capture and range of a Shotgun microphone.

- **MP3 recorder.** External MP3 recorders offer another alternative to the internal audio recording capabilities of DSLRs. These small, portable devices produce great audio that can easily be transferred through an inserted SDHC card. Many filmmakers like the mounting options for these devices. MP3 recorders can be attached to the top of the DSLR hot shoe mount or closer to the subject on a tripod or boom pole.

While recording on a separate device is great for audio quality, it requires an additional step in the final production stage. The audio and video files will need to be synchronized inside of your editing software. This is accomplished by cueing the video to the exact frame where the audio begins. The use of a tablet app that mimics the traditional clapper found at the beginning of raw movie videos can assist with the synchronization process.

- Mult box connection. Mult boxes offer unparalleled quality when capturing audio. A mult box, also known as a press box, contains multiple outputs of a single captured audio source such as onstage and shotgun microphones. The audio captured via a mult box runs through a mixer, operated by a sound engineer, before it goes to the output. Providing the sound engineer with the ability to manipulate the capture sound to compensate for noise produces a clean audio signal.

The highest quality sound is recorded when an HD camcorder or DSLR audio capture cables are plugged into the mult box. Mult boxes offer outputs in various formats, but the XLR format is the standard found in these devices. Best practice indicates that a 12- to 20-foot XLR cable should be available to connect to a mult box at events. In many cases, early arrival at a scheduled, professional shoot increases the chance that you will be able to connect to an available mult box. Sound engineers may unplug late arrivals from a mult box. Speak with a venue's sound engineer prior to a scheduled event when you're planning to access a mult box.

4.2.1.5 Mobile Device Video Recording

Improvements in lens technology have made it possible to capture usable videos and photographs with mobile devices such as iPhones and tablets. These mobile devices can be equipped with external lens and audio adapters to improve the quality of their sound and pictures. With these accessories, mobile devices can capture clear, crisp videos.

While technology is rapidly evolving and it is tempting to use a phone or tablet to capture video for planned social media or online promotion activities, mobile devices are not yet able to produce the professional-level videos created with DSLRs or HD camcorders. Consider mobile devices to be last-minute options, not primary capture sources. For short promotional videos—no more than two to five minutes in length—that will be viewed primarily on social media outlets such as Instagram, Facebook and Twitter, mobile devices can be used with the following recommendations.

Tips for Recording with a Mobile Device

There are several guides that outline techniques for capturing video with a mobile device. In summary, the guides identify four main areas that impact the quality of these videos:

1. **Stabilization.** Holding a mobile device when recording video will produce motion blur or distorted imaging affected by "rolling shutter." To keep the device steady, attach it to a stable tripod for still shots, or to a gimbal stabilizer for video.

2. **Image lighting.** Good lighting is required for quality video outputs. There are editing apps that can correct white balance and color correction when recording indoors. The use of an external LED light on a tripod can assist with shooting videos indoors. When shooting videos outside, avoid facing the camera toward the sun or placing subjects in areas that produce shadows.

3. **Audio capture.** Microphones on mobile devices do not have the same quality as DSLRs. This limitation can be bridged by combining the mobile device with a quality external microphone. Adapters can be purchased that allow for an external microphone, XLR cable or professional audio capture device to capture sound from the mobile device.

4. **Proximity to subject.** Mobile devices are not able to clearly capture images from a distance. It is recommended that the mobile device capture images from a stationary position no more than 10 feet from the subject. Shooting from a greater distance may produce blurry videos that require editing and cropping.

4.2.2 Develop a Video Plan

The key benefits of video are in creating connection, trust, authenticity and familiarity. The most effective videos combine visual, audio, appropriate music and text, so there is more reinforcement of the message and therefore better recall. Other key benefits of a short online video to demonstrate thought leadership include:

- It is one of the best ways to create visibility online, in part because many search engines are currently set to give preference to sites with video content
- It forces the subject to reduce his or her message to the essentials
- Rehearsals and retakes mean that it is possible to put one's best foot forward and to create a good first impression
- It shows the subject to be an early adopter, comfortable with new ideas

Video is not for the repeating of a résumé. A good video presentation includes a story that demonstrates the ideas in action. Avoid lists and jargon. While YouTube (or alternatives, such as Vimeo) may be a convenient place to post a video, it has its limitations. One is that the presenter has no control over where YouTube sends the viewer after the segment is complete—possibly to a competitor, or to a site with which you would not want to be associated. As well, the comments that viewers can place below the video may detract from the message. It's best to host a video on your own site.

When developing a video plan, consider the following:
- Key messages
- What words you're going to use (script)
- Who you're going to feature (actors)
- What you're going to film (what you want viewers to see)
- Intended response from target audience

Start by defining the key messages that you want the video to communicate. Are you trying to tell your audience that your firm is really good at using technology to build projects faster and cheaper? Are you sending a message to interns that they'll have a great career if they come to work at your firm? Keep in mind what the completed video will be used for (e.g., a documentary case study, testimonial or awards entry) throughout this process. The key messages and intended use define the video's audience.

Next you must decide how best to communicate that message. Here, you have a ton of creative freedom, so for the purposes of this section, let's assume that you've decided to use an interview format. Depending on what information you're looking for, you would have to then choose who to interview. Would a client or employee be the best subject, or should you turn to partners that you've worked on a project with (e.g., subcontractors, architects, engineers, user groups, etc.)? Remember that you also need to write dialogue to tell a story that puts the interview in context and includes any additional information that you want the viewer to know that isn't covered in the interview.

Other key considerations include imagery and tone. If you're making a video with the intention of recruiting interns or new full time employees, you want to make the viewer excited to come work for you. You might want to show people having fun in their daily work—people smiling, laughing, looking like they're contributing to the team—and highlight some of the coolest things that your firm is doing. However, if the video is intended to bring awareness to onsite safety, a more serious tone is appropriate for showing instances of what could happen if proper safety precautions aren't followed.

Flesh out these ideas and put them to paper with a storyboard. A storyboard is a series of drawings connected by dialogue and directions that outline the shots that you plan to include in the video. These drawings don't have to be works of art—photographs or stick figures are more than fine, as long as they represent exactly what you need to shoot. In conjunction with the script, the storyboard acts as a guide for what the final deliverable should look like at the end of the filming process. It should be as specific as possible, and include the names of the individuals that you need to tell the story or to engage with the topic, a list of locations that you plan to shoot at (and what you want to shoot while you're there), and a list of B-roll shots that will be used to fill the video in during editing.

B-roll shots are similar to stock photography. They're images that you've filmed previously (and you should be filming a lot of B-roll) and can use later during the editing process to fill in any gaps, connect one section to another, and give the video a more dynamic feel. Your B-roll list should be developed based on what you're trying to showcase. For example, in a video that will be shown to college students at a career fair, your B-roll might consist of a lot of action shots of employees having fun at work. People have a fairly short attention span, so B-rolls are a good way to break up long segments that might otherwise make your audience drift off. If you need to collect B-roll of something that you can't film yourself, such as aerial shots or footage from a location in another country, search through a service that provides stock B-roll footage, such as Beachfront B-Roll. A list of such services is provided in the Related Resources section.

In addition to the above considerations, the budget for your video will vary depending on the following factors:

- **Who's filming.** Hiring a videographer may seem expensive, but remember that they typically provide their own equipment. Filming the video yourself means that you'll need at least a camera, a tripod, lighting, microphones, lenses and maybe additional cameras for capturing different types of footage.
- **How the final deliverable will be used.** An award entry, for example, requires higher production value than a video that will only be seen by staff.
- **Length.** How long will it take to communicate your message? Videos cost more the longer they take to film.

Once you've determined your message, story and budget, develop a video capture plan that outlines these factors (otherwise known as the "four Ws:" who, what, where and why) and commit the project to a schedule.

4.2.3 Legal Issues

Review the copyright information related to video production to avoid infringement. These laws can differ slightly from state to state, so read up on what the rules are for your specific jurisdiction. In general, any people who appear in your video must sign a release form or contract that states clearly, in writing, that they give you permission to use their image. This paper should be signed and dated, and kept somewhere safe.

Pay attention to the licensing requirements of any music that you want to use in your video. Most songs have strict copyright restrictions, and if you use them outside of those stipulations (which often include some kind of payment) you could get into serious legal trouble. You can, however, use any music that is either royalty-free or within the public domain. Songs considered within the public domain are any published in 1922 or earlier, so you're fairly limited to orchestral pieces and folk songs. See the Related Resources section for more information on how to find royalty-free or public domain music.

4.3 Audio Podcasts

Just as commercial radio has continued to thrive despite competition from media that add visuals, audio podcasts have continued to be a popular way to absorb information. Podcasts are particularly useful when the visual component is not particularly important—a talking head works about as well in audio-only as it does if there's an image of the person talking. This means that they can be good for telling stories, as in a case study, one reason why audio books are more universal.

These advantages mean that podcasts are an excellent choice, in many cases, for distributing thought-leading content. Other advantages: Compared to video, it is relatively easy to produce professional-level results. Many third-party websites such as those of professional magazines and associations are willing to host audio podcasts, as they add to the amount of content on the site without adding unduly to the server load. As well, it is easy to produce a podcast from a telephone call, meaning that an interviewee in another location can be recorded easily.

The technology for creating a podcast is easier to understand than video; and it is easier to produce acceptable results with a minimum of skill and equipment—including the GarageBand program bundled with every Apple computer. Podcasts are good for topics where there is not a lot of value in adding the visual component—such as a straightforward "talking-head" presentation or speech. Podcasts can be hosted on your firm's website, distributed by social media such as Twitter and LinkedIn, and posted on public sharing sites such as digg.com.

 4.4 Key Terms

Below are the main terms covered in this section:
- Multimedia
- Viral videos
- Video plan
- Storyboard
- B-roll
- Release form
- Royalty-free
- Public domain
- Podcast

5 Coordinate Photography

While photography has been an essential communications tool in the marketing world for many years now, the costs of creating and distributing high-quality photographs that tell an exciting story have fallen dramatically. There is still a role for the professional photographer, but there are increasing opportunities for in-house involvement as well.

By the end of this section, you should understand the following key points, and be able to use them in your promotional activity work:

- The importance of documenting and maintaining a photographic record of key projects
- How to develop a broad portfolio of images for a variety of purposes
- The legal issues surrounding the use of images

5.1 Develop a Plan that Aligns with Marketing, BD and Strategic Plan Goals

Nothing tells your firm's story like good photographs. They are a window to your professional expertise that makes technical issues easier to understand and design concepts more emotionally appealing. They speak across all cultures and languages.

As a marketer, you are responsible for creating the best images to support your firm's marketing efforts. In a budget-less world, professional photographers would capture images of all of your firm's work fit to grace the covers of the industry's most prestigious magazines, and you could sit back and take all of the credit for making everyone look good. In reality, you probably have a limited budget for professional photography and will need to use additional resources such as internal and stock photography to provide tangible evidence of your firm's skills.

Depending on your firm's willingness to budget for photography, you will most likely be limited to a few projects per year that warrant the expense of hiring a professional. Spend your budget wisely by determining which projects will best showcase your firm's design skills and expertise and which projects best represent the markets you will be pursuing. In short, you must determine which images will give you the most return. This can be a difficult challenge when you are faced with several projects nearing completion simultaneously or with project managers who think that their project deserves to be professionally photographed. Use your best judgment. You know what works in your communications pieces and proposals. You know which images you are always scrambling to find.

This concern is especially relevant for larger firms that do hundreds of projects each year. It's impossible to get pictures of every single one of those projects, so you need to make a plan based on the following questions:

- Which projects are high-profile?
- What projects will you want to work on again?

- What kinds of projects do you have lined up for the future?
- Are you submitting a specific project for an award?
- Do you need examples of specific skills for proposals?

IDEA
Stretch your budget even further by capturing images that can be used to fulfill multiple marketing needs.

Develop a shot list—a tracking mechanism to plan and monitor your photography program. This can be as simple as a Microsoft Excel spreadsheet or Microsoft Word document that contains information about projects to be photographed. Indicate which projects should be photographed professionally and which internally. Collect and document input from staff to determine the scope of photos needed. Include anticipated project milestones, completion dates, client contact information, etc. Note any logistical details such as where to park, who to contact onsite, best time of day, etc. The data may be organized in numerous ways, such as chronologically by project completion date or by priority of photos needed. Photography completed can also be tracked to provide an overall image reference tool for developing marketing materials. Use this resource as a way to build and monitor the overall success of your program.

5.2 Identify Budget and Resources

Understand the photographer's costs (e.g., time, travel, digital post-production, etc.) and tailor your scope to your budget. Many marketers expect digital photography to cost less since there is no expense for film and development. However, these expenses have been replaced by the photographer's time spent retouching gigabytes of photographic data before the images are ready to process. Talk with your photographer about this process and decide if you need all images touched up or if you just want to select a few. While most photographers use digital equipment, some may prefer to still use film in environments that are less hospitable for sensitive digital equipment, such as dusty or muddy construction sites.

5.2.1 Photographing People

Featuring people in photographs is an effective way to emphasize the function of a project. Including a human element adds emotional appeal to your images and helps others relate to your work on a more personal level. Capturing your own staff in photos, either working together on job sites or in your office, can produce a unique and genuine reflection of your firm.

Feature people in photos to add emotional appeal and a human perspective to your work.

Keep in mind that working with people usually makes a photographer's job more difficult. Whether they are people actively using a facility, construction workers on a job site, or your own staff members with whom you have coordinated in advance to pose in the photos, make sure that you communicate to all what you are trying to accomplish. Discuss with your photographer what clothing colors and styles will work best for the images and advise your models accordingly. If you will be reproducing your images in one color only, you may want clothing combinations with high contrast. If you will be using your images in full color, you will need to be able to discern between color shades, even if they are all dark.

Choose your models wisely. Don't waste your time and budget with models that are going to fight the photographer. If you are using employees, be aware of their lasting effect on the image if they leave your firm. Photo releases should be obtained for all models. Initially, your models may lose their ability to look and act natural when they are in front of the camera. Be prepared to allow for a little giggle time. Make sure that they understand the amount of time involved.

Often people are unaware of the set-up time that photographers need to make lighting adjustments, lens changes, test photographs, etc. Don't ask someone to just drop in if they are going to be looking at their watch because what they perceived would take five minutes ends up being half an hour. Treat your models and your photographer fairly. You may just end up with some very genuine images that speak volumes about your firm.

5.2.2 Photographing Projects

Although marketers typically strive for a perfect photo that reveals an entire finished project in one dramatic image, photos taken during a project can be equally engaging. Construction images are excellent to use in proposals to demonstrate a particular service.

They provide a hands-on image of your firm's capabilities that is sometimes difficult to portray once the project is complete. Some projects, such as underground infrastructure, are only truly visible during construction. They can also work well in award submittals and other marketing materials that need to show a variety of images for one project. Before-and-after comparison photos can effectively show architectural and engineering accomplishments.

Capturing projects during construction can create dramatic images that show elements not visible after the project is complete.

Consider creating images that represent your firm's capabilities in a new way. Perhaps the most important thing to feature about a recently completed project isn't the project itself, but the end use. For instance, if your firm completed a major water improvement project, you could photograph the installation of the water mains during construction, the project area after completion or the nearby water treatment plant to which the mains lead. This approach would obviously demonstrate that your firm knows how to design and construct water mains. Another approach would be to photograph some children playing with a garden hose or running through a sprinkler. With the proper explanation, this image could be much more eye-catching and demonstrate that your firm understands the overall importance of clean water to the end-user. Brainstorm possible ideas and present them to your photographer. They may be able to create some of those images at a more leisurely pace and at a lower overall cost to you.

5.2.3 Stock Photos

Stock photography can be an effective part of your photography program, especially for those images that you don't have the time or budget to obtain any other way. For instance, if your firm is entering a new market where you don't have much experience to show, stock photos may be able to demonstrate your service or at least the end result. A wide variety of abstract imagery is available that can serve as design elements for your proposals and marketing materials. You may find other imagery that conveys a desired emotional appeal.

A wide variety of stock photography companies exist. Depending on the company, you can purchase a single image or an entire collection of images for unlimited use at a fairly reasonable price. The vast amount of imagery available can be easily browsed on the Internet. For a list of popular sites, see the Related Resources section.

Photographers hired to cover special events may be another source. If sporting or social events have taken place in the facilities that you have built, find out if a photographer was hired to capture that event. Many sell their photographs online. For example, a street restoration project in downtown Flint, MI, designed by Wade Trim, showcases the start of a world-class road race. An image purchased from the event photographer shows how the work projects a positive image to thousands of visitors each year.

With stock photography, keep in mind that any other company has access to the same images that you do. Consider whether you want to use a stock image in your higher-profile marketing materials. Are you comfortable with photos of models representing your own people? How will you feel if another company shows up at a trade show with the same image used on your exhibit?

5.3   Elements of a Strong Photo

Good photography depends on many factors: photographer's talent and equipment, cost, your ability to communicate what you want, project location, site constraints, weather, seasons, etc. Planning ahead can help you to make the most of each of these components to capture your best images.

Make sure that your project is ready to be photographed. What looks "finished" to others may not mean camera-ready to you. If possible, visit the site yourself to confirm that the landscaping is complete and all construction materials have been removed. For interior photography, plan a walk-through of the building to allow the photographer to meet with the designer, owner or other key people. Share a marked-up floor plan with the photographer that indicates what needs to be shot and identify any maintenance issues that need to be addressed. Discuss any issues related to site access, lighting, furniture and fixtures. Aesthetic distractions such as older furniture or poor landscaping will need to be dealt with creatively.

Consider removing trash cans or other incidental objects that can also detract from your image. Will the building be in use during the shoot? If not, how will issues like security, alarms and elevator use be handled? For exterior photography, provide the photographer with a site plan that indicates what needs to be shot. Address structure and property issues such as facility maintenance needs, landscaping, fountains, sprinkler systems and lighting. Determine if there are dumpsters, scaffolding, window stickers, fences, debris, graffiti or other elements that would detract from your photos. Don't let site location determine which projects get professionally photographed. The photographer's travel time may be cost-prohibitive for a single, distant site, but

Getting pictures of work in progress can be very powerful, but be careful when photographing sites encumbered with construction materials or other distractions.

DOMAIN 05

A photo-ready site will maximize the return on your photography investment.

you may be able to reduce costs by having several nearby projects photographed in the same day. It may also be more cost-effective to work with several photographers that are located near different projects. Site constraints may hinder a photographer's ability to capture good images. If your site is too difficult to access or just not worth the extra cost, consider others.

Take advantage of the seasons, whenever possible. Whether you desire the lush green of summer grass, a forested background of fall colors or a clean, snowy foreground, you can take advantage of seasonal dynamics with proper planning. Seasonal changes also include project use times. If you are photographing a golf course or other recreational facility, you may want to wait until people are actually using it to give your photos a human appeal. Or you may have an interior space that needs to be scheduled at a specific time when no one will be around to interfere with the shot. If you are going to spend the money for professional photography, make sure that your efforts are timed to give you the results that you desire. Keep in mind that good timing also means photographing a project early enough in its completion that it still appears clean and new. Waiting a year to photograph something just to catch a season can compromise the quality of your images in other ways.

Mother Nature does not care about your photography budget. If the site is to be shot outdoors, your photographer should be prepared for inclement weather. Good photographers book up quickly, so make sure that you select an alternative date when you are scheduling to get a second chance if the weather is miserable. Sometimes a not-so-sunny day can actually produce better images because your photographer doesn't have to contend with sunspots.

Consider the time of day. East- or west-facing structures should be shot early or late in the day for best detail. Building shadows can be very large and distracting at certain times of the day. Taking shots at dusk can be very dramatic. Determine if there is a specific time when your project will be in use or a special event taking place that you need to schedule for.

5.3.1 Taking the Photos Yourself

Getting behind the camera yourself can build a significant and valuable photographic library of your firm's work. Most marketers wear the photography hat at least some of the time, or work with others who are responsible for taking photos. If you don't have a basic knowledge of photography, consider taking a class or make "tagalongs" with your professional photographer a priority to learn from experience. Play around with the camera in site conditions similar to those you expect to be in to determine if any adjustments need to be made to the camera's settings.** While most of us probably use the camera's automatic settings, professional photographers will tell you that you will never get an optimal image using automatic settings.** Make sure that you have a good understanding of how to use your camera effectively to achieve your desired images before you get to the site.

Take advantage of other internal staff resources to expand your photograph collection efforts. Ask a project manager to snap a few shots on the next visit to the project site. Field or construction staff can also be an excellent source of photographs. Most projects are documented in photographs from beginning to end for internal records. While this is no guarantee that the images taken will be high quality or even usable for your marketing purposes, you may be pleasantly surprised by what you find. Staff may have captured an image of a critical area during construction of the project that you can no longer see. Take a look through the existing project photo files to determine if you already have usable images or to better prepare for going out to the site yourself.

Tips for Taking Your Own Pictures

- Use a tripod to stabilize the camera and get the clearest image possible.
- Determine the best time of day to shoot your subject and wait for the best possible day. Lighting is key.

- Take a lot of pictures to give yourself a wide variety to choose from.
- Experiment with different camera angles, including taking shots from high and low points.
- Fill the frame. Don't be afraid to get close to your subject.

Staff member portraits and group photos are often used in newsletters, proposals, news releases and other marketing activities. Consider whether these photos should be taken professionally or internally. A professional photographer can provide the proper lighting and backgrounds needed for a quality image but will be more costly and often require a longer lead time for a studio appointment. When working with a studio, make sure that you clearly understand your rights to use the images. Studios that focus more on personal rather than business clients often have strict limits on photography use that will need to be negotiated.

Some photographers may be willing to come to your office to take photos of your staff. This approach can reduce the burden on staff to go to a studio and may reduce costs if there are multiple subjects. Internal portrait photos can be taken quickly with minimal cost, but may not reflect the quality desired due to poor backgrounds and shadows. Choose an approach that best meets your objectives and implement it as consistently as possible so that your images will be complementary when used together. Like project photography, images of your staff should portray a memorable and positive image of your firm.

There are many benefits to taking your own photos. Greater flexibility allows you to change your photo shoot schedule to respond to weather conditions or other variables. Experiencing a project onsite is an excellent opportunity to expand your knowledge of the project and your firm's capabilities, while building relationships with field staff that may provide technical support when developing proposal or marketing materials. For projects that take longer to be ready for professional photography due to landscaping needs or other issues, taking photos yourself enables you to demonstrate the project experience in proposals or other materials while you are waiting for those professional shots.

5.4 Best Practices for Working with Architectural Photographers

There are many good professional photographers. To find one, ask other marketers who they have used and how their photographer worked with them. Contact professional associations in your industry, like the American Institute of Architects, to see which professional photographers are members. Ask your clients. They may have worked with photographers on other occasions or projects. Search the Internet. Most photographers have websites and online portfolios of their work. Magazines always feature professional photography. Look through current and old issues to find some photography that you like and track the photographer down from the photo credit. Look for image styles or projects that are similar to what you have in mind. Are you looking for a photographer that merely records your project in a well-focused photo, or are you looking for someone who may offer a more creative approach? Do you want someone who is easy to work with and open to your suggestions, or do you prefer someone with their own strong ideas on how and when to photograph a project?

Interview your photographer. Possessing digital camera technology does not make someone a professional photographer. Discuss what your expectations are and what kind of work they have done. Is the photographer a portrait photographer who does a little commercial work? Take the time to find someone who specializes in commercial work specific to your firm's services. Architecture, engineering and construction subjects require different photographic approaches. Do you need someone who specializes in photographing architecture and interior design or do you need someone who focuses more on the process and mechanical and electrical aspects of a structure? Does the photographer work well in construction environments where underground projects need to be captured?

Look through the photographer's portfolio for images that you like. Explain what in particular you like about the images or how the approach could be changed to meet your needs. Make sure that you are comfortable with the photographer's ability to handle the scope of your shoot. If you are shooting only interiors, be sure that they demonstrate the ability to handle lighting to create a natural appearance. Make sure that you are talking with the person who is going to take the photos. If your photographer is sending someone else out, you may want to think twice about using him or her, or have another meeting with the actual person who will be doing the shoot.

Guide your professional photographer with specific information about the images that you desire. There is no way for the photographer to know that you are dying for a close-up of a crane unless you say so. Do you want ground shots or aerials? Do you want people using the facility or do you want to focus on the space? Explain who your audience is and how the images will be used. Explain how many different images you are expecting.

TARGET POINT

If your subject is a one-time event such as a construction milestone, groundbreaking or dedication ceremony, make sure that the photographer understands that these images will never be able to be captured again so that they can prioritize your shoot accordingly.

Think about the major end uses for your images. Clarify specific issues such as time, budget, location and what digital file format the images need to be in. Determine what image resolution is needed. Shooting 8-inch-by-10-inch images at 300 dpi is a high resolution standard that should meet the majority of your needs. If you are going to enlarge the images for display purposes, higher-resolution images will give you the best results. The photographer should also shoot the images close to final size so that cropping will not compromise the quality of your print when enlarged.

Listen to your photographer's ideas. A skilled photographer looks for ways to enhance and emphasize the virtues of your project. They should have suggestions for camera

angles, props, composition and lighting. A soccer field that includes kids kicking a ball around provides greater impact than an empty field. For interior spaces, you may want to bring additional furniture or flowers to the site. Night photography can produce dramatic and refreshing images of building exteriors or a park that has lighting. It is important to give your photographer some room for creativity. Make sure that they get the exact images that you want and, budget provided, encourage him to play a bit on his own. Your photographer's eye may catch a unique perspective that you would have never thought to capture. You may find that these images are your favorites because of their ability to reveal something unique or creative about your project. The expense of a few more images once the photographer is onsite and set up is minor compared to the overall cost.

If possible, accompany your photographer on the shoot so that you can provide input on location. Often, a photographer will come up with new ideas onsite and may want your input as to whether or not you agree. If you are unable to attend the shoot, it may be helpful to take some of your own shots of the site before you meet with the photographer. This will allow you to point out specific areas that you want to feature and help the photographer better prepare for the shoot.

If you will not be present, make sure that your photographer has a confirmed contact person onsite, if needed. Your field people and those who are directly involved with the project are the best contacts. Most likely, these are the people who can best direct the photographer's efforts and coordinate any project scheduling issues. If your project is under construction, you may want a safety person onsite to make sure that no violations are photographed. Although the violation may be minor, the photographs will speak poorly of your firm and will most likely be unusable. It is best if the photographer speaks directly with the onsite contact to verify meeting time and location. If your photography shoot affects the project schedule, explain the importance of your photographer's mission to your personnel so that they are not frustrated and angry when they have to work around the photographer for a day.

Getting the Most from Your Photographer

- Plan ahead to allow ample time for a bad weather day or other variables.
- Clearly communicate what you expect the photos to feature and how they will be used. Make the day of the shoot as productive as possible: Prearrange site contacts, obtain client approval, confirm the project is ready, attend a walk-through and anticipate any other critical details that could waste the photographer's time onsite.
- Give the photographer creative license to show you what he or she does best.
- Join the photographer on the shoot to troubleshoot any unexpected issues, provide input as needed and expand your own photographic skills.
- Follow up with the photographer afterwards to discuss what you liked and what you would do differently next time.

5.5 Legal Issues

Understanding the proper legal use for professional and stock photography is critical. Even though you have the digital files in your possession, the original photographer still owns the copyright to the images that they created. Use of the photograph must be licensed to you through a licensing agreement that specifies who will use the images, how and where the images will appear and how long the images will be used. When hiring a professional photographer, you should agree on the scope of a license before photography has begun. If multiple licensees are involved, a written licensing agreement should be provided for each party. Likewise, stock photography companies will require you to sign a license agreement during your purchase that indicates that you agree to their terms of use.

As time passes, you may find that your original intent for image use has changed. Any changes in use that deviate from the original licensing agreement should be discussed with the photographer because they still hold the copyright to your image. Also, if you want to share images with others who were not involved in the commissioned assignment, permission must be obtained in writing from the photographer. If you receive images from another party and do not have written permission for their use, it is your responsibility to secure licensing rights before using them. Any copying, reproduction, distribution, public display or creation of derivative works of images without specific permission from the photographer is a violation of Federal copyright law.

Professional photographers should be credited for their work. Even after you have paid for the photography and bought the images, the photographer should be given credit in an appropriate manner. This does not mean that your new corporate brochure needs to have the photographer's name captioned all over the place. General practice is to include the photographer's credit line, usually printed on the work, in at least 6-point type alongside or near the photo. This helps the photographer to promote his or her work and makes your firm look professional. For stock photography, refer to your licensing agreement to determine if a credit is required.

Obtain client approval to photograph any project. An uninformed or unwilling client can put a stop to photography in a hurry. The client should be informed about when the photographer will be onsite. There may be sensitive photographic issues to consider for some clients, such as schools or churches. Most clients are proud of their facilities and will look forward to seeing their projects captured in images.

Be careful when manipulating your photographs post-shoot. A digital photograph can be manipulated through software programs such as Adobe Photoshop to achieve varied results. Consider using these techniques to lengthen the usable life of your images. For instance, you could apply different filters to the same image to achieve drastically different looks. The more you use one particular image, the less overall impact it will have. If you are forced to shoot a subject before it is ready, digital manipulation can help. Unwanted scaffolding or a construction barrel can be removed. Green grass can be added to a sparse area or a gray sky can be made blue to improve your image. Be aware that digital manipulation has raised serious legal and ethical questions. Architecture and engineering firms are advised to use good judgment

when manipulating photos. Changing the color of the sky or making other alterations to simply improve the image is acceptable. Altering the façade of a building or adding details that vary from the actual structure is not. Take care not to make changes that lower the integrity of your image.

Keep it Legal

- Define terms of use for photos using a written licensing agreement with the photographer
- Notify the photographer of any changes in your intent to use photos
- Obtain written permission from the photographer to use photos acquired through another source
- Include photographer credit line when image is published
- Don't compromise the integrity of your photos through digital manipulation

 ## 5.6 Key Terms

Below are the main terms covered in this section:

- Shot list
- Stock photography
- Licensing agreement

6 Prepare Award Competition Entries

Winning an award can be an important benchmark and a strategic advantage relative to where your firm stands among peers. It can be a morale boost, and it can lead to greater visibility and new engagements. For that reason, entering an award competition should be treated as seriously as many other business ventures.

By the end of this section, you should understand the following key points, and be able to use them in your promotional activity work:

- The potential value to your company of entering and winning award competitions
- How to identify an appropriate competition to enter, and determine the likelihood of winning
- How to prepare your entry, and how to allocate the necessary resources

6.1 Why Enter?

You should allocate some time, resources and a small amount of your annual marketing budget for awards campaigns. You don't need to spend a fortune here (perhaps one to two percent of your overall budget would be enough). For larger practices, this allocation could include selected "pay-to-play" entries, where you purchase advertising or are ready to absorb significant entry and/or awards banquet fees for significant client-focused competitions.

Awards are difficult things for which to calculate a definite ROI. Several SMPS members say that awards programs are profitable and useful, but that they cannot directly link their awards success with actual BD results and profitability. Arguably, the greatest advantage of awards programs is the combination of improved staff morale and enhanced client relationships.

With awards programs, there is often an awards ceremony or event. Clients are often invited to these events—that gives them a chance to showcase their project and receive recognition for a job well done. Of course, awards banquets are also an ideal opportunity for marketers and business developers to spend some high-value time with clients after the projects have been completed, building the base for future work and enthusiastic testimonials and referrals.

Awards program success can be measured through determining how it has influenced perceptions of your firm, information that can be gleaned from survey data. Additionally, awards programs overall add to ongoing efforts to position the firm as a leader in a competitive marketplace. Third-party endorsement can have a positive impact. Some industry rankings include awards won as a metric. For example, the Top 50 Architects list, published annually by ARCHITECT Magazine, weighs design awards. Finally, the awards submissions are a great team-building tool and are great for recruitment and retention efforts.

As all awards programs have their own specific and varied criteria for entry and winning, it's a difficult topic to dig into the minutiae of how best to prepare your entry

for each one in a section of this length. You'll have to do research on each of the competitions that you want to enter to understand precisely what is required of you. For the rest of this section, we will focus on a broader view of how to find competitions that suit your firm and the basic skills that you'll need to know to pursue any award.

6.2 Track Award Opportunities

Identify awards that you want to chase based on project type, market type and the relevancy of the project. Create a system (it could be as basic as a Microsoft Excel spreadsheet) to keep track of award opportunities and update it on an annual basis. Awards opportunities can be found by contacting A/E/C associations, reading relevant publications, and reaching out to your community.

For example, within SMPS's Marketer publication, you'll find brief descriptions of four awards programs that recognize the best and brightest leaders in professional services marketing and the Society:

1. **Marketing Communications Awards.** MCA is the oldest and most prestigious industry awards program, recognizing excellence in marketing communications by professional services firms in the fields of architecture, engineering and construction. The 20+ competition categories range from books and brochures, to media relations, newsletters, videos and websites.

2. **Weld Coxe Marketing Achievement Award.** The Society's highest honor salutes a remarkable marketing or BD professional for significant and measurable accomplishments in research, education, professional leadership, marketing communications and innovative programs.

3. **Fellows Recognition Program.** SMPS recognizes—with the designation of Fellow (FSMPS)—longstanding, certified members who have made significant contributions to the profession and the Society.

4. **Chapter Award.** The Striving for Excellence and Chapter President of the Year awards honor dedicated volunteers and their chapters for extraordinary leadership and service to members.

More information about entry details and deadlines can be found on the Recognition tab on www.smps.org.

6.3 Determine Likelihood of Winning Award

Once you've identified award programs that you'd like to enter, ask yourself: Could we actually win this? Is our project likely to be the best? You should only enter a competition if you think that you have a good chance of winning and if the entry truly reflects your best work. A well-researched go/no-go process is essential. Scrutinize the award criteria against your project and come up with an honest, objective opinion of your firm's ability to win.

Start with a review of past winners—if you're able to, look up the actual entries. SMPS keeps a record of winning entries, and other organizations are likely to as well. How does your entry compare? Reach out to past winners and members of the jury to get more detailed insight into what judges are looking for. Ask them what made the difference between winning and losing, and what mistakes you should take care to avoid.

If the host of the award has shared the names of the present jury, learn a little about them. Read their blogs and articles (especially those that they've written on the topic of your proposed entry), research the firm they work for, etc. What is their background? What market sector/industry/geography is their expertise based in? Ultimately, you should gather enough information to answer the most important question: How likely are they to appreciate your entry? Will they fall in love with your project? Name it the winner?

If you think that your project stands a good chance of winning the award, prepare an entry that will stand out from the competition. In general, a good award submission will include the following elements:

- A good relationship with the clients of the project that you want to submit
- Stunning visuals
- A story told from a creative and unique angle
- Relevance to the project award criteria of that particular awards program

The jury will consider every entry through the lens of one main question: "Why should we care?" Your submission must convince viewers that your project is important, and why. Identify all of the benefits that your project created—to the client, to the environment, to the industry and to the community—and do so in a way that is both clear and engaging. No one can resist a good story, so tell one. Translate your project into a narrative complete with characters (you, your client), conflict (your client's problem, risks faced should the project fail) and resolution (what you learned, how it turned out).

6.4   Include Visuals

Awards competitions are visually driven events—they often exist to provide compelling content for the host's magazine or annual conferences—so great visuals are one of the most important factors in winning. Invest in professional photography, and make complex planning, architecture and construction outcomes easy to understand through the use of well-designed graphics.

Floor plans, site plans, photos of the finished product, tables and graphs, etc., should all be jury-ready and in a publishable format. Use these graphic elements as a narrative device throughout your entry. They should help to tell the story of your project, fitting seamlessly into the narrative flow. Make sure to leave plenty of white space to make the visuals pop and the text easy to read.

6.5 Include the Voice of the Client in the Award Narrative

The client's perspective is what will give your entry dimension. Interview the client and solicit comments about how satisfied they were with the solution that your firm provided. Ask them to comment specifically on how the solution helped their company to increase revenue, improve productivity, recruit talent or improve client experience. Place these quotes directly into the award submission narrative, and, if possible, include a testimonial letter as well.

Client quotes can lend a sense of urgency to the content (e.g., "If the arena wasn't built by February, we would have been in hot water."), and energize the voice of the story. Testimonials provide a way to brag about your firm's performance without doing it yourself.

6.6 Budget Time and Resources for Editing, Proofing, Etc.

Put as much effort into an awards presentation as you would an RFP or client presentation. Take care to understand the rules and criteria, and then design your entry to be as appealing as possible to the judges. Make sure that you have enough time to write multiple drafts—finding a distinct voice for your story sometimes takes a ton of editing, rewriting and polishing, but it's essential to differentiate your entry from other, more plainly written submissions. Juries reading entry after entry of dry, perfunctory text will be delighted to come across a story with panache.

IDEA

Hire a proofreader to look for typos and any inconsistencies in grammar or font. The simplest of errors can pull a reader out of the story and distract from the message that you want to impart.

Most important of all: Start early! Give yourself plenty of time to throw away drafts, find better materials and interview busy clients. Lengthy preparation will often account for the difference between a loss and a win.

 ## 6.7 Key Terms

Below are the main terms covered in this section:

- Awards campaign
- Jury

7 Develop an Advertising Plan

Advertising is transformed by the digital revolution that we are living in as consumers. Yet the purpose of advertising remains the same: to raise awareness of your company in the minds of prospective clients.

By the end of this section, you should understand the following key points, and be able to use them in your promotional activity work:

- The importance of knowing exactly what and why you are advertising
- How different types of advertising can be used to achieve different goals

7.1 Establish an Advertising Rationale

Before embarking on an advertising campaign, a professional service firm should examine all avenues for promotion to determine whether advertising is the best way to get its message delivered to its target markets. Advertising is only one element of the marketing program and should be consistent with the objectives of the overall marketing program—brand positioning, image and strategy. A systematic approach to planning and strategy should be employed. Advertising should be well conceived, planned and executed.

In general, firms consider advertising when entering a new market, launching a new service or expanding into a new geographic region where they are not well-known. The recent emergence of pay-to-play advertising (which will be discussed in detail later in this section) has expanded this list to include situations when paying to get your firm featured in a client-read publication is the best way to get in front of a target audience.

Another consideration to take into account is whether you are in a market that is primarily fee-driven or merit-driven. Fee-driven markets are those in which firms are selling based on price. All of the firms vying for a project make a bid, and in most cases the buyer picks a bid based on price. Many construction firms, for example, are bid-based. In this type of market, there's less reason to advertise because there's not much need for a firm to communicate its differentiator and value proposition—it all comes down to fee. If this is the market that your firm operates within, you probably won't have much of an advertising budget anyway, since you're trying to keep your bid low. In a merit-driven market, however, firms are selected for a job based on their expertise, and they negotiate a fee after being chosen. Advertising is more important within this type of market.

Other factors that will impact the decision to advertise include:

- **Cost.** Is an advertising campaign within your firm's budget? Will a particular campaign bring in more money than it costs?
- **Client presence.** Does your target audience read the magazine in which you're thinking of placing an ad? Are actual clients included in the subscriber base of the publication?

> **TARGET POINT**
>
> Be careful when evaluating your audience. Avoid ad vehicles that are seen primarily by other professional service firms as opposed to clients. Many trade publications that are design- or construction-oriented, for example, are seen much more by builders and constructors than by owners.

Advertising is expensive—it's important to develop a plan that will give you the highest ROI. Make sure that your ads are placed in a platform that is read by people in the position to hire or recommend A/E/C service professionals. An ad seen by a million people isn't helpful if none of them have connections to your market. In general, advertisements in trade publications and directory ads for professional organizations that firms support are good places to start. Make your selection from these based on which outlet has the readers, listeners, users or viewers that best match your target audience and has the most credibility.

> **TARGET POINT**
> **Finding an Audience**
>
> EKP Consulting Engineers, Inc. just opened an office in Bozeman, MT and needs to let construction companies know that they've arrived. They decide to place an ad in one of the five real estate journals that operate in the area, and do some research on each publications' readership, distribution, content and editorial calendar.
>
> They found a real estate journal that reaches the audience that they want to target, and features different markets for each edition. They choose the editions that align with their markets and customize their ads accordingly.
>
> Over time, EKP notices an increase in Bozeman-area visitors to their website during the week the journal comes out, so, in addition to customizing their ad for the market focus, they also begin to update their social media accounts and website home page with images and content related to that market.
>
> **Key Concepts for this Story:**
> - Careful research can help you to identify the best advertising vehicle to reach your target market, and the right message to pique their interest
> - Advertising should be just one element of an integrated communications effort

7.2 Relate Goals and Target Audience to Your Overall Marketing Plan

As with any marketing program, promotional campaign, or PR program, you have to begin with the basics. Objectives must be clearly defined, ads must be well-planned and designed, and the media chosen wisely. Consider these key questions:

- What do you want to accomplish? (objective)
- Who do you wish to reach? (market)
- What do you wish to convey? (message)
- Which is the best format for conveying the message? (medium)
- What can you afford to spend? (budget)
- How will you know that it worked? (evaluation)

Once it is determined that the use of advertising will allow the professional service firm to fulfill its objective, a plan is developed. The plan can be simple, but should consist of the following elements:

- Objective
- Audience
- Message
- Medium (from categories listed below)
- Budget
- Who is to manage
- Expectations and time frame (frequency and coverage)
- Evaluation

As we discussed before, be highly selective in placing your ads. Once you've chosen a platform, place your ads there as frequently as possible to ensure the highest impact. Repetition is key.

In The New How to Advertise, Roman and Maas state that advertising must be delivered with sufficient frequency to be effective. People have short memories. They forget 60 percent of what they learn within half a day, so there's not much value in one-time buys. The more repetitive a message is, the better it will be retained. Advertisers who seek to reach a broad audience at the expense of sufficient frequency among key prospects risk wasting much of the investment.

A case can also be made for impact—concentrating everything on a dramatic program that rises above the clutter and commands attention, rather than spreading it over a long period of time. It's a seductive concept that relies on the hope that people will remember. Studies by the Advertising Research Foundation and the Association of Business Publishers, by Alfred Politz Media Studies, and by W. R. Simmons & Associates Research, conclude, "It's clear that creating a strong message is only a start. The more you repeat it, the stronger it gets."

7.3 Different Types of Ads and Sponsorships

The world of advertising has certainly changed since the days of brochures. Now, with social networks making it easy to find and share information about firms and services, the advertising process is much more inbound. Firms write stories to capture the

interest of their markets, put those stories into the digital world and use the techniques discussed in section 4 ("Establishing a Web Presence") to help people find them. The idea is that by finding these stories, your audience will learn something new or share them with someone else.

That said, there are still different types of advertising that can be utilized to enable a firm to fulfill its objectives. The following three types of media contain the different categories of advertising that will be discussed later in this section:

1. **Earned.** Publicity your firm earns by having a great story or entertaining feature. Includes stories submitted to publications, research submitted to journals and most awards competitions (discussed further in section 9). Not to be confused with pay-to-play ads disguised as earned ads.

2. **Paid.** An advertisement that your firm pays a platform to host. Includes advertorials; PBS underwriting; and institutional, service and broadcast advertising.

3. **Owned.** Content produced and published by your firm and put up on your own website/blog. Includes tombstone ads and social media advertising.

7.3.1 Institutional or Image Advertising

Institutional ads are designed solely to enhance the name recognition or reputation of a firm without focusing on a specific service. For example, a civil engineering firm used a series of ads that played on the name of the firm. The ads featured an interesting visual—a cow with zebra stripes, for instance—and a headline that read, "Unique approaches to environmental problems." The firm was not really selling a particular benefit, but attempting to generate name recognition in its target market. Institutional advertising is useful, but should not be used to generate immediate new business. It does, however, have its place as part of a larger campaign.

7.3.2 Service Advertising

This includes display or promotional advertising in which a service or capability is described in a selling context. These are highly focused ads that describe a particular service to a clearly defined audience. For example, a consultant who specializes in selling a marketing management database program to architectural firms would use this kind of advertising.

7.3.3 Tombstone Advertisements

Tombstone ads are simple, straightforward announcements. They are used to announce a significant event like a merger, major personnel change, acquisition or new office. It is one additional technique to provide visibility for a firm or to convey an impression to prospective clients. These days, this type of ad is typically presented as an announcement over a firm's website and social media account, or via an HTML email.

7.3.4 Broadcast Advertising

These are ads placed on radio and television, and are not generally used by A/E/C firms because the specialized nature of this industry offers no guarantee that the many people who see or hear these ads will include prospective clients.

7.3.5 Advertorials

Advertorials are a mixture of advertisement and editorial content. Many magazines and newspapers—from the New York Times to the local daily paper—have some version of this, where a firm pays the publication to write an article about them that is seen by readers as editorial content (e.g., as news as opposed to an ad). Pay-to-play advertising is exploding right now because as the more traditional types of advertising dry up, publishers have to find another way to make enough money to stay afloat.

Here is an example of how this type of advertising often works:

A man calls your office and says, "Hi, I'm an editor with Sustainable Design magazine and I came across your firm online. You look like a really interesting company, and we'd like to profile you in our next issue." At first, this seems like an example of earned advertising, but don't confuse the two. In this type, when you talk with the editor and learn more details, you find that there's a fee or some other kind of quid pro quo involved.

7.3.6 Social Media Advertising

Social media is a great, free way to reach out to your audience and share information about your firm. Advertisements about upcoming projects, new personnel, forays into a new market and any other updates that you want your followers to know about can be shared at the click of a button. We discussed social media in more depth in section 4, and the tips from that section can be easily applied to online advertising.

7.3.7 PBS Underwriting

Every city has a PBS radio and TV station which advertises through their sponsors. At the top of the hour, after a program ends, an announcer will say, "We'd like to thank our underwriters…" and include the names of people and firms that sponsored their content. Sometimes they will include a little blurb about your firm, and this blurb is recognized by listeners as an ad.

 7.4 Key Terms

Below are the main terms covered in this section:

- Advertising plan
- Fee-driven market
- Merit-driven market
- Earned advertising
- Owned advertising
- Institutional/image advertisements
- Service advertisements
- Tombstone advertisements
- Broadcast advertisements
- Pay-to-play advertising

8 Plan Trade Show Activities and Conference Speaking

Trade shows and conference engagements are among the many ways to get your company's message out in front of a wider audience. But you'll need to plan your activities wisely to make sure that the return on your significant investment—in both money and time—are worth it.

By the end of this section, you should understand the following key points, and be able to use them in your promotional activity work:

- How to choose the proper venue to reach your target audience
- How to select the best way to present your firm at different venues
- How to match the level of engagement with the expected ROI

8.1 Decide Whether to Participate

8.1.1 Types of Trade Shows/Conferences

Many associations have discovered that a good way to raise money and provide exposure for their sponsors or associate members is to host a trade show in conjunction with their conference. Exhibit halls can be found at all types of conferences, even regional and local chapters of professional associations. Traffic through exhibit halls is reflective of the association's efforts to bring attendees to the area and of the overall tone of the conference.

Selecting trade shows that provide face-to-face opportunities with decision-makers and influencers in your target market is critical to achieving an ROI. Trade shows should be evaluated on a yearly basis to determine whether or not they provide enough marketing and lead generation opportunities. Just because your firm exhibited last year, it doesn't mean that you need to exhibit the following year.

Evaluate the show objectively. Are you connecting with clients? Are the attendees decision-makers or can they influence the decision-making process? Do attendees seem interested in the exhibit area or do they avoid it? Does the association promote traffic in the exhibit area? Are there enough exhibit hours to justify the effort of setting up and breaking down the display? Are conference sessions held in the same building as the exhibit hall? Are half of the other exhibitor consultants offering the same services as your firm? Are more of the exhibitors suppliers of equipment and products, creating a different feel at the show? Would your firm stand out more if you sponsored a conference activity instead of an exhibit? Is this a conference of your peers where staff would be more effective networking as attendees? Would a hospitality suite allow you to meet your objectives better than a booth? If you exhibited last year, did you meet your objectives? Why or why not?

If it is a show that you have never attended, ask for a list of the previous year's exhibitors and attendees with titles. Contact a few exhibitors and ask what they

thought of the show. Are they planning on exhibiting again this year? What were their marketing objectives last year and did they meet them? If you're still not sure or if it's a first time show, don't exhibit. Attend the show and spend some time in the exhibit area talking to attendees and exhibitors to see how the show is going. Make your decision to exhibit the following year based on this feedback.

When selecting shows, also consider what other marketing and BD activities will be going on around the same time. Frequently, trade show seasons emerge within industries, where a one-month or two-month period becomes crowded with shows. Several back-to-back trade shows can stress resources; prioritize events so that staff members aren't stretched too thin.

Trade shows in public and private markets can also provide very different opportunities. Associations for public sector clients—like local government, regional government, utilities and schools—can provide opportunities to meet with elected officials who are not always easy to reach. These shows can also provide access to an entire group of decision-makers and influencers. While targeted clients don't typically travel in packs, you can organize activities outside of the exhibit area and touch multiple decision-makers with the same client throughout the day. This can be particularly valuable when you are triangulating to confirm the validity of information. Specialty conferences within these markets can provide access to higher-level decision-makers and deliver better networking opportunities.

Some trade shows in the private sector can offer stronger traditional lead development opportunities. Frequently in private markets, there are fewer decision-makers involved in hiring consultants and the selection process is faster, so relationships can yield results more quickly.

Other trade shows provide the opportunity to support a state association in which your clients are actively involved. Clients may expect you to exhibit at these shows—a valid reason to have a booth.

IDEA
Consider your goals in relation to a particular conference's market. If your goal is to hit a million dollars in new fee sales for healthcare work over the next year, does it make sense to attend a wind show conference? Spend your money and resources in the places that you're trying to make money.

Once you decide to exhibit, send in the exhibit contract and payment right away. Many shows have online registration to facilitate the process. If your exhibit contract includes additional items such as advertising, name badges or other requests that you haven't decided on yet, don't let that delay your contract submission. Submit those items later on. Some shows sell out quickly and booths are frequently assigned on a first-come, first-served basis.

8.1.2 Align Your Goals with Trade show/Conference Opportunities

Aligning your goals with a particular trade show or conference is a necessary part of the planning process. What do you most want to gain through attending? Examples of goals that you might focus on include:

- Thought leadership—establishing yourself as an authority on relevant topics by delivering the answers to the biggest questions on the minds of your target audience
- Client prospecting
- Relationship building
- Identifying competitors
- Establishing your firm's brand

Identifying your goals will help you to determine on which parts of the conference you should focus your energy.

Some metrics to measure that may help you to calculate your ROI include:

- Identifying new projects
- Project team introductions to clients/partners
- Gathering competitive data
- Media/PR outreach
- Education
- Client outreach

Knowing your market and targeting activities toward it is the key to trade-show success. Why do attendees come to the show? Do they come because of the great networking opportunities to learn what their peers are doing? Or because the show is always held at a great location with lots of opportunities for sightseeing or golf? If you don't know, find out. If it is the latter, don't exhibit. Consider hosting a special event or sponsoring a part of the conference and having your staff network.

Does the exhibit hall appeal to your senses at every turn? Are interactive exhibits the norm, where attendees come for a little entertainment? If yes, build an interactive component into your exhibit. Borrow ideas from pop culture and the entertainment industry, but take the time to make ideas relevant to your services. You want visitors to have fun and remember the experience; more importantly, you want visitors to remember your firm.

If it truly is an educational show where others come to learn about advances in the field and what their peers are doing, focus on this in your exhibit. Find something meaningful that booth visitors can walk away with that is relevant to their search.

Sharing research findings about funding mechanisms or energy-saving techniques that schools are employing would be more meaningful than a glow-in-the-dark Frisbee in this type of environment. Establish yourself as an expert in a specific area.

Don't limit your market to attendees. Are any of the exhibitors clients? Or can they potentially provide referrals for your firm? Make a point of talking with them and giving them valuable information. The hosting association should also be viewed as a potential client. Introduce yourself to the staff organizing the event. They always like to connect a face with a voice on the telephone. Once you've established a relationship, they might turn to you when they need an article for their association's publication or a speaker for a seminar. Give association staff honest feedback on how the show is going, offer specific suggestions of how to improve something you are not happy about and let them know when things have gone smoothly because of their behind-the-scenes work.

Email and social media are helpful in promoting your trade show activities before the event. Tie your message in with the theme of your exhibit and offer an incentive to stop by the booth. The incentive could be a report, a giveaway, or a chance to win a prize. Your website is another way to promote your exhibit ahead of time. Websites offer the added benefit of providing a means of post-show communications and bringing potential clients back to your site after the show. If you are conducting an informal survey at the show, tell everyone that you will be posting the results on your website in two weeks.

8.2   Develop a Budget

The costs of a trade show booth include staff time, graphics, carpet/padding, electronics, electricity, giveaway items, travel, shipping, other miscellaneous expenses and often the cost of buying space on the showroom floor. Some conferences charge a registration fee, and some will comp that fee if you are one of the speakers. However, the cost of being a speaker includes the time you spend writing, outlining and practicing your speech. This opportunity cost may negate what you save in registration fees.

Other costs to consider are travel (how far you will have to drive/fly to get to the venue) and lodging.

8.3   Craft a Plan of Engagement

8.3.1   Choose Your Speaker's Topic

Speaking at a session builds firm credibility with the association sponsoring the conference and attendees. Be sure to focus on an area of expertise, not your firm.

Choose a topic that:

- **Is relevant to your audience.** Make sure that most people there will be able to relate to and learn from your presentation. If you're speaking at a healthcare conference, talk about the NIC unit that your firm built last year.

- **Aligns with your marketing and BD goals.** Whose attention and business are you looking to gain?

- **Is something that you want to work on again.** Ideally, your session will generate excitement about the topic, and will result in your firm being hired to do more work in that area.

Say that your firm has been hired to renovate Daytona International Speedway. Even if you attend a sports-related conference, there are not many clients across the country that build speedways of that magnitude, so pitching a topic titled "How to Build the Best Speedway" isn't likely to generate much interest. However, the new technologies that you're using to construct the speedway faster and more efficiently will appeal to firms in almost any market. Don't limit your influence by choosing too narrow of a topic.

IDEA

Leave a written summary of your session for attendees to take with them when they leave. Keep copies in your booth afterwards and post it on your website as well.

8.3.2 Identify the Appropriate Participants for your Booth

People are the most memorable part of an exhibit. Interacting with company employees gives booth visitors a more realistic glimpse of the company. Because they aren't edited, proofed and mass-produced, employees truly depict the brand of a company. Use this to your advantage! A knowledgeable, trained booth staff member can differentiate your firm from the competition.

Train all staff who will participate in trade show activities once per year. If everyone is experienced, hold a meeting to brainstorm ways to improve booth performance and enhance the firm's image at the show. Review your trade show plan and budget and explain how each person can help achieve marketing objectives. Assess the previous year's performance in terms of number of clients/targeted clients touched, quality of discussions and competitor activities. Even seasoned marketers benefit from sharing ideas and having a refresher course on exhibit-floor selling. Set up programs for experienced staff to mentor new staff. More can be learned from spending a few hours with a skilled exhibitor than from hearing or reading about it.

Above all, make sure that staff members are trained in communications skills. Most of us are not accustomed to daily "full body" selling; learning how to pick up on nonverbal cues is very important. Numerous studies have revealed that staff behavior is remembered most about an exhibit and that most of the information received from the conversation is nonverbal. As obvious as it sounds, using body language that demonstrates that you are at the show to talk to attendees and listen to their concerns is important. It is always amazing to see the number of exhibitors eating in their booth, eagerly chatting with their exhibit neighbor, talking on a cell phone, or just sitting there looking completely disinterested. Why would anyone want to stop and talk to them, even if they had the best looking exhibit at the show?

When selecting staff to work the exhibit, consider a mix of technical and marketing staff. Marketing staff know clients and recognize client names, while technical staff

validates specialized expertise to potential clients. Each staff member at the booth should be outgoing and able to talk knowledgeably about the services that you provide, past projects, and what your firm has to offer that distinguishes it from others.

With a 10-by-10-foot booth area, it's ideal to have at least three staffers, so that there are always two people manning the booth while the third person is on break, attending sessions, meeting with clients, or checking out the competition. If you have an interactive component to your exhibit that requires staff attention to keep it going, dedicate one or two staff members to the interactive component and have two other people available to talk with visitors when they complete the activity or while they are waiting their turn.

Most firms have staff wear business-casual attire with shirts imprinted with their company logo. This allows visitors to quickly identify staff working the booth and allows staff to be comfortable throughout a long day.

8.3.3 Constructing a Display

The keys to an effective exhibit are strong graphics, a concise message and talented people. Each is dependent on the others.

Trade show graphics have one purpose—to communicate your message. The challenge includes making the message brief, yet bold enough to grab attention and be memorable. The adage "less is more" really applies here. If you have a 10-by10-foot booth space, most trade-show attendees will take three to five seconds as they are approaching your booth to understand who you are, what you do, and what you can do for THEM. This is not the time or place to display a laundry list of your features and benefits—that should be done in handouts and pre- and post-show marketing, and perhaps as secondary signage within your booth. One clear message combined with a "stop them in their tracks" visual will cause most attendees to pause long enough in front of your booth for your staffers to check out badges and engage them in conversation.

When developing a message for your exhibit, keep it simple. The exhibit should clearly demonstrate how your firm can help convention attendees. Remember, they are looking for solutions to their problems, not company names and logos. Show how your service relates to their needs. Do your homework. The exhibit should demonstrate your understanding of the market. Look at every component of your exhibit to see how it can be used to help achieve your objectives.

There are a variety of portable display structures to display your message. Many professional service firms favor display structures covered in Velcro receptive fabric. This allows the opportunity to display a changeable selection of photos highlighting clients' projects. When selecting the color of the fabric backgrounds, consider what types of photographs and graphics that you will be putting on them. Black, gray and neutral colors are best for a variety of image types, including outdoor images, schematics or maps.

All printed panels should be readable from at least eight to 12 feet away, the distance from the edge of the aisle to your display. People generally don't read text below kneecap level, so keep any important text above it. If you don't have a graphic designer on staff, work with one from your display supplier. A professionally designed display will always make a more positive impact than if you try to design it yourself.

Using full-color printed fabric panels instead of rigid panels for your messaging is very popular, as exhibitors prefer displays that are easy to use and transport. One current trend is to use display walls composed of your graphics printed on one large piece of fabric that stays attached to the frame. These are referred to as "pop-ups" because they instantly pop up from their collapsed, compact structure. Pop-ups remain very popular because they are lightweight and quick and easy to set up. If you are looking for the opportunity to change some of your graphic panels for different audiences, there are pop-ups that allow for this kind of customization by utilizing small fabric panels attached to the frame that can be affordably changed out as needed, while still keeping a unified look to your display. Another popular trend is to create a lightweight, easy-to-setup display wall composed of side-by-side banner stands. With the right design, you can change the messaging to reach different audiences by swapping out banners rather than creating a whole new display wall graphic.

Tabletop displays have remained popular over the years. Most exhibiting venues provide exhibitors with a six- or eight-foot black or white skirted table, although you may choose to reinforce your brand by using a table "throw" (an unfitted table cloth) with your logo in your corporate colors. Putting your tabletop display on top of the table will usually put it at the same height as a freestanding wall display, and you're not paying for all of the extra structure and graphics. However, keep in mind that in the common "bigger is better" mindset, using a tabletop display may make your company appear smaller than those using full wall displays. Some firms purchase tabletop displays for tabletop-only shows or to use for sponsorship opportunities at local meetings.

If you are purchasing a portable display, evaluate several different manufacturers before you select a model. Set each one up by yourself to see how easy assembly is. Look at the number of cases required and the cost of shipping them. Will your display fit into a car or do you need an SUV or van? Is it easy to set up? Will it damage easily if it is shipped or not packed properly? (Don't assume that staff will follow the packing instructions to the letter.) Is it easy to update the images on the front if you need to create different looks for different shows? How do the electrical cords come together in the back? Decide what features are important enough to guide your decision-making. If you are still not sure about purchasing a specific display, see if you can rent it. If you like it, you may be able to purchase it after the show for a discounted price.

Be cautious about purchasing a display through an Internet auction site or a discount website. The display you receive may not look as good as the picture or description. You don't want to discover two weeks before a show that the frame that you bought didn't come with connectors and the seller doesn't know where they are. Nothing beats having a display professional assist you in getting the display that best fits your needs with no surprises. Reputable exhibit and display suppliers back their products and assist their clients in making sure that they have covered the details.

The size and amount of time required to assemble a display should also be considered during your purchase. Some exhibit halls require the use of union labor to set up and break down displays that require tools (even an Allen wrench). Associations will send you to a website listing all of the requirements for installation and dismantling (referred to as I&D). One note of caution: The general show contractor or decorator may not give your display the level of attention that an independent I&D company would. Ask your display provider to furnish you with recommended firms or ask them to arrange the I&D for you.

Most standard 10-foot displays can be quickly and easily set up by one or two booth staffers. Setup for simple displays, such as two adjoining 10-foot booths that require contract labor to install, can typically be accomplished in one or two hours, with less time needed for teardown.

A display will last if it is properly cared for. The fewer people handling it, the better. Take the time to pull your exhibit out at least once per year and check it out thoroughly to see if it needs any repairs and if any pieces are missing. Consider sending your display back to the manufacturer for refurbishing if it is looking a little battered but still has a few good years left in it. Recognize when an exhibit has met the end of its useful life and replace it. Sometimes you can get away with replacing the graphic panels to push the purchase off until next year's budget. Use good judgment—a run-down display presents a run-down image.

8.3.4 Level of Presence

Determining the level of presence that you want your firm to have at a show is dependent on what business you're trying to drum up, what markets you want to enter and what clients you want to pull in. Understand who is going to be at the show that you're attending, and how much money you're willing to spend to get the attention of that audience. Take into consideration your marketing plan, sales goals, the potential ROI and how many members of your firm will be attending. If only one person is going, it makes no sense to buy the biggest booth on the trade show floor.

8.4 Gather Information and Follow Up

Trade shows are about networking, and the exhibit hall isn't the only place to do it. Frequently, better networking opportunities exist outside of the exhibit hall.

Hosting a client dinner or hospitality suite offers the opportunity to meet with clients and potential clients in an informal setting. If you have a large number of clients attending the conference, a client dinner may be more effective. The exclusivity of a client-only reception can also be beneficial. Be sure to invite clients three to four weeks ahead of time so that they can plan appropriately. Client dinners can become an annual event that clients cherish over the years. These dinners can also be tied to local sporting events and tourist attractions. They are also a great way to say thank you to your clients and let them know that you value their work in an environment where they are surrounded by your competitors.

Depending on past history and the number of other hospitality suites at a conference, a firm can get lost in the crowd. If convention attendees hop from room to room, they may not pay attention to whose hospitality suite they are in. Talk with conference organizers to find out how many other suites there will be and what days and times they will be held. Ask the hotel what type of food is being planned in other rooms so that you don't have the same menu. Consider just desserts, a martini bar, or some other theme to make your room stand out. If possible, check out the suite or room ahead of time, particularly if you have a choice of rooms. Consider how many employees are available to work the room when setting the hours. Don't have the person closing the hospitality room work the morning shift in the booth the next day.

Trade shows aren't over when the exhibits are dismantled. Issues and upcoming projects discussed with clients and potential clients require a timely follow up. Studies indicate that trade show recall drops after eight weeks and that leads should be followed up within 30 days.

Before the show is over, determine how follow up will be conducted, who will do it and when it will be done. Have people following up document the results. Also, keep track of which clients you talked with, who you took out to eat or who came to your dinner or hospitality suite.

8.5   Evaluate ROI Post-Show

Don't forget to debrief with your staff while the trade show is still fresh in their minds. Have someone who was not involved in planning the show conduct short telephone or email surveys to get their thoughts on the show. Generally, you will get more candid feedback over the phone than from a written evaluation form. Ask what they thought about the conference as a whole. Was it well-attended? What type of image did the firm project? Did clients stop by? What did they say? Which activities provided the best opportunities for networking? Were attendees aware of your sponsorship? Was the booth easy to work out of? Did attendees understand the theme? How could the booth have been improved? Should your company have a booth next year? What were competitors doing? Was the hospitality room effective? Were your marketing objectives met?

If you didn't meet your exhibit objectives, find out why. Was it due to improper show selection? Booth location? Booth personnel problems? Poorly designed exhibit? Poor follow up? Low show attendance? Similarly, if you did meet your objectives, find out why. Carefully consider employee and convention attendee suggestions and be open to modifying future approaches.

For conferences where you give presentations, ROI can be determined with questions that relate to how much continued exposure your speech generated. If your goal was to generate press from the speaking opportunity, did it succeed? Was there something written about you in a newspaper? Did someone from the press contact you for more information? Did someone come up to schedule a meeting with you after your talk? Were there one or five articles written about you? How many people connected with you because you spoke? Were you mentioned over social media?

Many associations request feedback from exhibitors after the show. Take time to fill out their survey and provide constructive feedback about the positive and negative aspects of your exhibit experience.

 8.6 Key Terms

Below are the main terms covered in this section:
- Trade show
- Exhibit hall
- Thought leader

9 Coordinate Firm Special Events

There are many ways that you can showcase the special nature of your firm; perhaps none will convey the firm's vitality better than the special event. Here is where planning and creativity can come together to create a favorable lasting impression in the minds of your target audience.

By the end of this section, you should understand the following key points, and be able to use them in your promotional activity work:

- The importance of careful planning in identifying the why, what, how and who of the event
- How to pick a central theme for the event that ties in with your corporate branding
- How to evaluate the event and calculate the ROI

9.1 Plan the Event

What are special events? Are they open houses or groundbreakings? Are they dinners or meetings? Are they anniversaries or holidays? Are they parties or ceremonies?

Any of these situations, and many others, could be turned into a special event for your organization. The recipe for making any of these situations special will require a careful sifting of your objectives, a large helping of knowledge about what stimulates your target audience and a dash of creativity. When it works, a lasting positive impression, based on the unique characteristics of your organization, will be permanently etched on the minds of your prospects.

If executed correctly, special events can cast a light on an organization's human side, personalize the organization, pull it off of the printed page and out of the office building and reveal its character and vitality. Along with targeted direct-mail campaigns, fancy brochures and other PR staples, a creative special event can reach new prospects and old clients and engage them in a way that will put your organization in a special place on the critical "bidders" list that your future client maintains.

Whether you are counting on five guests or 5,000, the secret of successful special events lies in planning. The following steps are a general roadmap for successful events.

9.1.1 Define Your Goals

Decide why you are planning the special event in the first place. What do you hope to realize as a result of this event? Two weeks after the event, what one thing do you want your prospects to remember about your firm? For example, you might answer, "We want our clients and prospects to remember that we are the fastest growing A/E firm in town." Your goals need to be specific and clear. If your primary goal cannot be stated in a short sentence, you are not focused enough. Consider the SMART acronym (specific, measurable, attainable, relevant and time-bound) in testing how well you have articulated your event goals.

Remember that special events are only one piece of the overall PR and marketing communications program. In fact, special events should be a standard part of your yearly PR/marketing plan. Whatever the focus of your communications program is, that will probably lead your special events.

Of course, special event goals should be based on a careful review of your organization's concerns and marketing objectives. Does a particular market sector need bolstering? Will there be a new service introduced in the year ahead? If so, how should you handle its introduction? If you plan your marketing around market segments, special events can follow. Should you offer a seminar for your clients or prospects? How about spicing up that old hospitality suite so it does more than give your prospects a free drink?

Timing is also crucial. Thus, it is important to develop a yearly plan of special events. This also provides sufficient lead time for the detailed planning required to execute an event properly. If the event is planned to coincide with other significant happenings, its impact may be greatly increased or decreased depending on the circumstances. For example, Christmas parties are great but tend to blend with all of the other holiday parties, while a party on St. Patrick's Day will probably stand out.

9.1.2 Identify Your Audience

Tailor your event to suit the common interests, personal needs, age and disposition of those you invite. Determine what these people already know about you. What other means of communication have you used to approach them? What are their current impressions of your organization? Before you begin to think about the content of the program, develop an accurate list of prospects and group or individual profiles.

You may want to plan the event for some segment of your overall audience. An event targeted at a healthcare audience, as an example, may generate a larger benefit than trying to talk to the total list of prospects for the company. Remember, each client thinks that his or her business is unique and has different problems than everyone else in the world. With a segmented group, it is much easier to find ways to stimulate a select set of needs or interests.

In some cases, the audience can be as select as an individual client. Typically, 20 percent of your clients bring 80 percent of your work. Doing something special for these folks continues to build the relationship and, in most cases, people like doing business with people they know and trust.

Don't forget that not only do your clients and prospects want to talk to you; they want to talk to each other. Social networking should be an element of the way that you look at the event. In fact, your target audience will be more willing to come if they think that they will have an opportunity to network with each other.

9.1.3 Develop the Central Concept

Decide what aspect of your services or specific capabilities relates most to the audience that you are trying to reach. If your event satisfies some special need for your audience, you have the beginnings of a really special event. Ask yourself the question, "If I were a prospect, why would I come to this event? What do I get out of the event?" If your answer is, "Gosh, I don't know," you have work to do.

You can plan a party, and many of your existing clients may come, but what will attract the prospect that has been reluctant to give you the time of day? Take the example of one firm that sponsored an ice cream social as part of its annual open house. They served a large variety of ice cream—except there was no vanilla. They tied the event to the theme, "We don't do vanilla architecture." That ice cream social stimulates more interest than a bland announcement that XYZ is having an open house at its new office, and it drives home a theme that positions the firm with its clients.

TARGET POINT

Is your firm a champagne or a beer-bucket kind of firm? Are you classical music or rock and roll? Your event should reflect your firm's personality.

Remember that your firm has knowledge that your clients want. Share that knowledge. Show your clients how to improve their operations. There are firms that are afraid to give away information to their clients. The fact is, if clients think that they can take your discussion and not use your services, working for them would have been a disaster anyway. The smart clients will see you as an expert and want to retain you. When you can give clients information that helps them do their jobs better, they keep it and refer to it, and you will get those unexpected phone calls when they need your help.

9.1.4 Give it the Creative Sparkle

The average American is bombarded with more than 1,800 competing advertising messages each day. Professional services firms, unfortunately, must battle all of them for equal time. So you must find ways to capture the attention of your audience—from the invitation to the thank you.

Your prime prospects are busy people who probably receive dozens of invitations to similar events throughout the year. To catch their attention, something about your event must be more appealing, innovative or useful to them than what they would normally do with their time.

The difference between an event and a special event is that a special event employs those elements and approaches that satisfy audience needs and captures their interest. The truly special event presents these benefits to the audience in an unusual way. This is the point where you must apply creativity to the basic concept. Making your events stand out from your prospects' daily routine is what will deliver your company's message effectively. Part of this process is to take risks. New ideas or different approaches generate interest.

The trick is to be innovative without doing something that looks frivolous or foolish. For example, a leading engineering firm buys a special performance of the local symphony orchestra and invites clients and prospects and their "significant others" for a classy evening. This event is not only fun, it matches the level of sophistication that the large diverse firm wants to exude. On the other hand, a smaller, trendy design boutique architect recently bought out one of the opening-day showings of a major new motion picture at a local theater and took its entire staff and clients.

Note how the vanilla architecture example mentioned earlier starts to add new dimension and communications opportunities. The realm of possibilities for creative promotional strategies is tremendous. The tie between architecture and ice cream is the creative sparkle needed to make the event memorable.

Special Events that Work

- **Hold a technical seminar.** Explain how to do what you do. Provide lunch or dinner. Some firms run mini-conferences and charge clients to attend. Offer to a very select list of clients and prospects. Some firms do this on an annual basis with industry updates, so that people look forward to the meeting each year.
- **Sponsor something—an award, a charity or a professional organization—and develop an event around it.**
- **Do something in conjunction with a conference or professional meeting.** Sponsor a breakfast, lunch or dinner with or without a special speaker. Host a party. Promote the event with the organization sponsoring the conference. Don't forget media tie-ins.
- **Do a "GREEN" event.** Team up with the U.S. Green Building Council (USGBC) and their local chapters. Find unusual ways to celebrate Earth Day. Your open house will be remembered longer if you have a theme.
- **Tie your event to a local or regional historic event.** Consider sending attendees of your event a follow-up package that links your communications themes with the event. Clients tend to keep interesting three-dimensional items or advertising specialties on credenzas.

9.2 Check, then Double Check

You can't get through most successful special events without a checklist. This applies whether you are preparing a preliminary budget, making sure that everything is arranged, or writing a post-event evaluation. Start with the event itself and work backward to prepare a detailed timetable for all elements. This checklist/schedule will become the cornerstone of your planning. Make sure that you list every activity and task that must be accomplished, who is responsible for implementation and when it has to be done. Then ask yourself, "What if?" By developing contingency plans and adding them to your checklist, you will eliminate a considerable amount of hassle, headaches and high blood pressure. During the execution of the event, you will have the ability to track all of the little details and make sure that everything comes together in the right place at the right time.

9.3 Post Event

After the dust settles, you need to analyze how things turned out. What went well and what could have been handled better? Did you achieve your communications and marketing goals? If not, why not? Do you want to do a similar event next year? How would you change that event based on what you learned for this event? Make sure any post-event mailers and follow ups are handled in a timely manner. Then start the planning for the next event.

A firm's image (good or bad) is developed over time. Its image can also change over time. One event will never tell a firm's whole story to a group of individuals, nor will a successful format be appropriate to follow over and over again for an extended period of time. Annual events can be done in such a way that clients and prospects look forward to them every year and anticipate receiving the announcement for the next occasion. The trick is to do these annual events with a new twist or flair so that they do not become stale and so that they continue to push your ever-evolving communications agenda.

In order to develop a truly communicative marketing program, you will need to re-evaluate your prime prospects continually. Things change. The marketplace, the economic environment and the outlook and concerns of your clients change as a result. Redefine your communications goals based on the needs and concerns of your clients. Study the components of your business and marketing plans further and find more creative ways to tell your story to your prospects. Special events can be a successful component to help you to tell your firm's story.

9.4 Other Corporate Entertainment Strategies

Entertaining clients includes everything from planning a party where you invite everyone you've done business with over the past year, to taking one client that you want to get closer to out to lunch. While not always a "special event," corporate entertainment strategies deserve a quick mention here. Section 2 goes into more detail about best practices for entertaining at a conference or trade show.

Your entertainment strategy must be tied to your overall sales plan, and depends heavily on your budget for BD activities. You only have a certain amount of money to spend on wining and dining clients, so it's important to make sure that you're spending it in the right place, and with the right people. The exact amount your firm makes available for corporate entertainment will vary widely according to its size, BD plan and current relationship with clients. The main reason for taking out clients is to build a relationship with them and win work for your firm, so make sure that the money that you spend ultimately brings you closer to achieving your firm's goals. Here are some tips for spending your entertainment budget wisely:

- Don't spend your entire budget on one client—choose events that won't bust the bank

- Allocate more funds to clients who have a ton of work sitting on the table, and especially to those whose work you know you would get a good return on
- Manage your money based on what kind of work you're chasing
- Choose a venue where you'll be able to spend quality time with your guest—a restaurant is a better choice than a metal concert (unless you happen to know that this particular client prefers mosh pits to meeting rooms)

Your entertainment strategy will also be very dependent on your clients' preferences and market sector, and the location that you work in, as each market and geography has different expectations and rule. Public sector employees, for example, are prohibited from accepting gifts, so offering to take a government client to lunch would not be appropriate. Understand the rules that govern the sectors that you operate within.

TARGET POINT
Maintenance vs Growth

Rita is in charge of corporate entertainment for Raymond Design, a firm that used to specialize in healthcare, but now wants to move into the energy sector. Every year, the firm attends a national healthcare trade show. In the past, Rita has made sure that Raymond Design had a big presence—she set up an interactive display in a highly trafficked area, presented a talk during the conference and invited 10 select clients out to an expensive dinner on the last day. The cost of all of this (including $2,000 spent at dinner) was worth the $2 million in new work that these activities brought in through improved relationships.

But this year, Raymond Design has allocated most of its BD budget towards building relationships with clients in the energy industry. Rita attends the healthcare trade show to maintain ties to that marketplace—Raymond Design is still finishing up a healthcare project and they're open to picking up another—but she doesn't try to make the splash that her firm has been known for in the past. Her team does not bring a display this year; and while Rita listens to the conference speakers, she doesn't prepare a presentation of her own. Instead of organizing a private dinner, she takes just one person out to lunch.

The goal this year was merely to avoid burning bridges, not to build new ones. Rita decides to save her time and resources for planning a big entrance into the energy conference happening next month in Toledo.

Key Concepts for this Story:
- Spending your entertainment dollars is a zero-sum game: Money spent in one area won't be available for growing business in another
- Make sure that your entertainment expenses align with your business objectives; keep in mind the ROI

 **9.5 Key Terms**

Below are the main terms covered in this section:
- Special events
- Corporate entertainment strategies

10 Select Vendors and Consultants

Consultants will be brought in from time to time, either for their specific expertise or simply to provide an extra set of hands at a critical time. The selection and management of consultants does not have to be a headache; by setting clear expectations and benchmarks, a consulting engagement can be a win-win for all.

By the end of this section, you should understand the following key points, and be able to use them in your promotional activity work:

- How to align a consultant's work with the business objectives of the company
- How to choose the best consultant for the job at hand
- How best to work with the consultant to attain your objectives

10.1 Define the Scope of Work

At some time, all companies engage consultants to support their business. In marketing and BD, this typically involves engagement of consultants to team with in pursuit of work, as well as hiring and managing consultants to support in-house functions such as PR, website development, writing, photography and graphic design.

Before you begin your search for a consultant, professional advisor or vendor, be sure that you know exactly what it is that you want to accomplish by working with a third party. Identify and define the problem that you are having or need that must be met and be able to articulate it clearly. How will you know that this problem has been solved? What will it look like when the need has been met? What changes would show the anticipated degree of improvement? A well-defined scope of work clearly states what services and outcomes are expected from the consultant. In making this investment of time upfront, you are setting the stage for a successful outcome.

In preparing the scope of work, avoid generalities and presumptions that will hinder the ability of the consultant to perform the work. If the scope of work seems vague, you should clarify the expectations for performance and the metrics used to evaluate the result. If your internal organization structure is bureaucratic (i.e., the work is being managed by the marketing department for some other department's use), specify the requirement to communicate extensively with the end-users to ensure that the project meets their desired result.

If the project budget is set, determine if the funding is based on a current and relevant estimate or modeled after a similar project. If the schedule is established, it is important to verify that the completion date is realistic. Do you have design standards from prior work that the consultant will be expected to apply to this project? Are there any implied liabilities for the performance of the work that are outside of the norm? Are there contractual methods established to deal with changes to the scope or schedule? If the contract is awarded based on technical qualifications only, take a proactive approach in establishing the value of the consulting fees by defining your own estimate for the project.

Your standards of quality for the project may not be the same as your consultant's. Thus, it becomes extraordinarily important that the initial communication between you and the consultant establishes and defines deliverables and the metrics that will be used for measuring the success of the completed project. Contracts based on a clear understanding of expectation are complete and include protections from the vagaries of less-than-clear desires on the part of the client.

Also assess whether the project for which you are procuring consultant services is in alignment with the company's strategic agenda and will not compete for time, funds or staff with other projects. Otherwise, both the consultants and your staff assigned to the project will become frustrated and costly hours will be wasted.

By setting the scope of work upfront and ensuring that the internal resources are in place to support your objective and need for hiring a consultant, your selection and management of consultants should proceed smoothly.

10.2 Select and Interview Vendors and Consultants

There are several methods for selecting a consultant. Single-source selection is justified when there is one consultant who clearly stands out with the special skills required for the project. This also applies when time constraints make it impractical to have an extensive search process. Often there is one consultant who is familiar with the specifics of the project who can create the potential for substantial cost savings, or, by the unique location of the project, save travel costs and be more cost-effective.

On larger, more complex projects, more often than not, the negotiated contract is the preferred method for consultant selection. This means a qualifications-based consultant selection vs. selection on price. As many of us have experienced in other aspects of our professional and personal lives, the lowest initial cost is typically not the lowest cost by the end of the project, nor the greatest value in regards to desired results. If all of the firms under consideration are capable of doing the work, then they should be interviewed, their references checked and their proposals evaluated against the selection criteria and available budget. The careful preparation of objectives prior to the proposal call will make this evaluation easier and fairer and will enable selection of the best proposal.

When a limited and select number of firms compete for the job, they are more likely to spend the time and effort on a more creative approach. The careful preparation of objectives prior to the proposal call will make evaluation easier and fairer and will enable selection of the best proposal.

The primary emphasis should always be on professional and technical merit. Provided all proposals are in a reasonable range, cost should play a relatively small role. Professional and technical competence has far-reaching and major financial implications well beyond the assignment itself. The evaluation process should never be a contest of experience or cost alone.

> **TARGET POINT**
> Hire the best consultant or vendor that you can afford—not just the cheapest—and don't be afraid to get a second opinion.

If you are engaging a firm instead of sole practitioner, ask who your account manager will be and meet with them. In this case, you are interviewing individuals, since a firm is no more and no less than the individuals assigned to your project. Ask how they will ensure that the account manager will stay on your project from inception through completion.

For larger, longer-term contracts, in addition to selection of the submittals and interviews, conduct a visit to the consultants' offices to assess their working style and resources. For example, in one selection process, a consultant submitted a thorough proposal and ensured that the resources were available to meet the scope of work. However, in touring this consultant's offices, it was evident that while they had a large office, there were many empty workstations.

Further, in asking a few people in residence, they said that they were interns called in for that day. The reality was, that while they claimed sufficient staff to meet the project objectives, it was clear that they had significantly downsized and that their capacity to meet the scope along with their other client commitments was not sufficient.

While you should take a disciplined selection approach based on pre-defined qualifications, when all other required attributes are equal, then personalities do come into play in selecting the right consultant. It is always a safer bet to work with a consultant that you have worked with successfully before since they are already familiar with your company and operating procedures. If they are all previously unproven consultants, then ask yourself the following questions: Which consultant do you feel most comfortable with? Which consultant will provide the client service in a manner conducive to your needs? And, which consultant do you believe that you will create the best partnership with as you work together to meet the project objective?

Some common-sense considerations in developing a list of consulting resources include:

- **Expertise.** Look for consultants who have specific experience in the type of project that you are undertaking. Selecting the firm that has specific experience assists in marketing the team and minimizes the learning curve during production. Ask your peers in other firms for referrals (and ask with whom they wouldn't work and why). Look at the consultants included in the teams of published projects that are similar to the work that your firm does.

- **References.** Ask for them and check them. Ask for current references that are relevant to the project that you are undertaking. If possible, ask the potential client whom they would recommend using. Ask others in your firm for their opinions of the consultant.

- **Key project personnel.** Ask for the names of the individuals who worked on the projects that are relevant to your project. Some consultants promote work produced by people who are no longer on staff. Others will solicit your work with experienced staff and assign someone else to the project once it is underway. Get written confirmation that those individuals will commit a specified amount of time to your project. Request their current and projected workloads. Minimize the potential of being handed off by asking these questions and getting commitments prior to project startup.
- **Financial stability.** Check the consultant's financial status and stability, years in business, and so on. More than once, a consultant firm has gone out of business or has gone bankrupt at a critical juncture in project development.
- **Exclusivity.** When selecting consultants for your team in pursuit of a project, determine whether they will team with your company on an exclusive basis. If the project is in-house and is a differentiator for your company (e.g., PR), then see if they are willing to agree to not work with competing companies. If they don't agree, then, at a minimum, request that the personnel assigned to your project not work with competing firms; also have them sign a confidentiality agreement.

In summary, the key to selecting the best consultant for your specific objectives lies in knowing the right questions to ask.

10.3 Manage and Direct Activities of Consultants

Once you have selected the consultant and signed the contract, invest in partnering with your consultant. This involves a meeting to introduce key members from both the consultant's and your firm's staff, reviewing the structure of the contracted relationship, and sharing background information on your company including the structure, services, experiences and company and marketing goals. Making this investment upfront will provide context for the consultant that will result in a better outcome.

You should also use the initial partnering session to define a system to communicate while the project is in progress. It is critical that both you and the consultant communicate consistently during the project's development. It is usually recommended that project communication happen a minimum of five times (at 20 percent completion milestones) to ensure that the project stays on track. Follow up each meeting with a memo documenting your understanding of the actions required, deadlines, presumed costs and major decisions so that there can be no room for confusion or error.

If a project is long in duration, multiple partnering sessions at regular intervals may be beneficial. These meetings are primarily to assess project status, but also to determine means of continuous improvement.

When hiring consultants, remember that you are the client. If you apply the same considerations and procedures in hiring a consultant that you would like your clients to use in selecting your firm, you can improve the consulting experience. Look at this process as an educational opportunity to learn how your firm can better position itself to be selected.

To have a successful consultant relationship, stay involved. Like your personal physician, your consultants can only know how to help if you communicate and share responsibility with them. If you do, you should have fewer horror stories and many conclusions that are more successful.

Find firms and people to work with whom you like and respect and who like and respect you. Consultants are professionals and react and perform best when they are treated with mutual respect. When you are in a stressful situation, it helps to know that everyone is doing their best and working toward the common goal. Socializing professionally with your regular consultants is a simple investment that can greatly enhance the collaborative effort. Good consultants interact with many clients and can be a wealth of competitive information and market research.

 ## 10.4 Key Terms

Below are the main terms covered in this section:

- Consultant
- Scope of work
- Deliverable
- Single-source selection

11 Case Study Activity

This Case Study Activity allows you to reflect on and apply the key concepts that you learned in this Domain to a real-world scenario. Each Domain includes a scenario about the same organization, Gilmore & Associates. The scenario is presented to you, followed by several questions. You can also elect to view the recommended solutions/responses for each question posed, which are located on the next page.

This case study can be used in many ways:

- You can individually reflect on the questions after reading the scenario, and write your own notes/responses to each question. You can then check your ability to apply the key concepts against the recommended solutions/responses.
- You can pull together a small group and use this scenario to drive a discussion around the challenge and to discuss solutions as a group.
- You can combine a selection of the case study activities (across the Domains) into a larger scenario-based activity as a part of a professional development event.

Gilmore & Associates' first year in the new market has been a successful one—with two winning proposals and one completed project, you are ready to get your company's message out in front of a wider audience. Your CEO wants the firm to become well-known for designing state-of-the-art facilities for serving the healthcare needs of older adults.

As the marketing coordinator, you have been given the responsibility of developing a plan to raise awareness of your company in the minds of prospective clients, and to set the stage for establishing your firm as a thought leader in the industry.

1. Before you engage in promotional activities, you must have a message to deliver. What are the elements involved in the creation of a corporate identity?

2. What activities should be included in the communications plan that your team develops?

3. You've decided to create a video to gain your firm more visibility. What should you keep in mind when developing/filming a high-quality multimedia advertisement?

4. Your firm is proud of the project that it recently completed, and would like to give it greater visibility by entering it into an awards competition. What should you consider when searching for an appropriate competition to submit to?

5. The first year anniversary of your company's entry into the new market is coming up, and you want to plan a special event for the occasion. What steps can you take to ensure that the event makes a favorable lasting impression on potential and current clients?

Answer Key

1. Before you engage in promotional activities, you must have a message to deliver. What are the elements involved in the creation of a corporate identity?

    o Conducting primary research to determine how your brand is currently viewed by others (i.e., a perception survey)

    o Determining whether others' perceptions of your company lines up with the image that you want to project

    o Developing a vision and mission statement that defines your firm's core purpose

    o Creating an identity map to determine where your firm stands in relation to your competitors in the market

    o Developing a corporate identity program that institutes firm-wide standards regarding naming conventions, graphic design elements and messaging in order to better maintain a consistent brand

2. What activities should be included in the communications plan that your team develops?

    o Creating strategic objectives that set the priorities and direction for communicating with clients, potential clients, the community and other key audiences. What response are you looking for?

    o Defining your target audience, based on demographic and psychographic characteristics.

    o Developing a social media plan that uses inbound marketing to engage with your audience on the appropriate platforms.

    o Developing interesting and creative content that can be used to share knowledge through various social, digital, and analog platforms.

    o Maintaining an integrated website.

    o Selecting which types of ads and sponsorships to engage in (including earned, pay-to-play, and owned platforms).

3. You've decided to create a video to gain your firm more visibility. What should you keep in mind when developing/filming a high-quality multimedia advertisement?

    o Tell a story, but make sure that it includes only what is essential so that the entire story can be told in a few minutes.

- Make sure that the quality of the production is consistent with your firm's overall image.

- Research the elements of video production and decide what tools you will need to produce the quality that you want. This includes finding a DSLR camera/camcorder with the right specs, deciding what frame rate/resolution it should be able to shoot at, and what type of microphone to use to capture sound.

4. Your firm is proud of the project that it recently completed, and would like to give it greater visibility by entering it into an awards competition. What should you consider when searching for an appropriate competition to submit to?

    - What are your next opportunities for entering an awards competition? Create a system to keep track of awards opportunities, and update it with information gathered by contacting A/E/C associations, reading relevant publications and reaching out to your network.

    - Does your project meet the criteria of that particular awards program?

    - Will winning the award boost your firm's visibility in your target market/audience?

    - Do you have a good chance of winning the competition? Review the past winners and compare them (objectively) against your own project.

5. The first year anniversary of your company's entry into the new market is coming up, and you want to plan a special event for the occasion. What steps can you take to ensure that the event makes a favorable lasting impression on potential and current clients?

    - Clearly define your goals for hosting the event before you begin planning it.

    - Develop a creative concept that represents your firm's personality and appeals to your target audience.

    - Create a checklist of every activity and task that must be accomplished both before and during the event, along with who is responsible for implementation. Include contingency plans for anything that might go wrong.

12 Glossary

301 Redirect
A piece of code on a website that tells the server that a page has moved to a new web address.

Advertising Plan
A plan that describes when, where and how advertisements will be used to best accomplish a firm's marketing goals.

Advertorial
A mixture between an advertisement and an article, an advertorial is produced when a firm pays a publication to write a positive article about them and pass it off as editorial.

Analytics
The study of business data using statistical analysis in order to discover and understand historical patterns to proactively predict and improve business performance in the future.

Awards Campaign
The plan developed by a firm that outlines the pursuit of a particular award.

Brand
The perceptions that audiences have of your product or service based upon their sum total of experiences with you, whether branding, marketing or operations.

Brand Architecture
The hierarchy and relationship structure between a parent brand and its sub-brands, divisions, departments, joint ventures, partnerships and affiliations.

Broadcast Advertisements
Advertisements placed on radio and television.

B-Roll
Video footage that has been filmed previously (or found on a stock footage website) and is added into a video during editing.

Communications Objectives
Measurable targets that help you to isolate which parts of your communications plan are working and which are not. They are created based on the responses that you desire from your target audience.

Communications Plan
A written document that describes what you want to accomplish with your communications, ways in which those objectives can be accomplished, to whom the communications will be addressed, how you will accomplish your objectives and how you will measure the results.

Consultant
Experienced professional who provides expert knowledge for a fee. He or she most often works in an advisory capacity, thus the A/E/C firm and its leaders retain responsibility for outcomes.

Content Calendar
A calendar that outlines all of the types of content that you will produce over a period of time. It includes the goals of the content to be shared, the topics for the content, who the content is targeting, who the author is, how the content will be distributed and deadlines and publication dates.

Corporate Entertainment Strategies
Entertainment hosted by your firm with the goal of building a relationship with clients.

Corporate Identity
The symbolic embodiment of a company, product or service, represented through images and ideas.

Corporate Identity Guidelines
Rules contained within a manual that outline how to use (and how not to use) the company logo and associated elements of your corporate identity in order to ensure brand consistency.

Deliverable
The consultant's output or contribution.

Demographic Characteristics
Attributes that can be measured or quantified.

Differentiation
The ways in which a product, service or firm is different from its competitors.

Earned Advertising
Publicity that your firm earns by having a great story or entertaining feature. Includes stories submitted to publications, research submitted to journals and most awards competitions.

Editorial Calendar
A schedule that outlines the theme for each issue of a publication.

Exhibit Hall
Area within a hotel or conference center where the exhibits are located.

Fee-Driven Market
Markets in which all firms vying for a project make a bid; and in most cases, the buyer picks a bid based on price.

Google Analytics
A partially free service provided by Google that reveals information on how people use your website and tells you how your website is performing compared to every other website out there.

Identity Map
A tool used to explore how your firm compares with your competitors.

Inbound Marketing
The practice of participating in a dialogue with clients through social media, content sharing and other tools.

Institutional/Image Advertisements
Advertisements designed solely to enhance the name recognition or reputation of a firm without focusing on a specific service.

Integration
The act of incorporating social media into your firm's website.

Jury
The panel of judges in charge of determining the winner of an awards competition.

Keyword
A word or phrase commonly entered into a search engine to find a particular product or service.

Licensing Agreement
A legal agreement granting permission to exercise specified rights to a work.

Merit-Driven Market
A market in which firms are selected for a job based on their expertise, and they negotiate a fee after being chosen.

Mission Statement
A statement that describes the direction in which your firm is headed.

Multimedia
Electronic media.

Naming Conventions
A formal structure and guidelines used to create brand names.

News Release
A public relations (PR) announcement issued to the news media and to other targeted publications for the purpose of letting the public know of company developments.

Outbound Marketing
Traditional advertising campaigns where a firm sends out information about their services to a potential client.

Owned Advertising

Advertisements produced and published by your firm and put up on your own website/blog. Includes tombstone ads and social media advertising.

Pay-to-Play Advertising
Advertisements that your firm pays a platform to host. Includes advertorials; PBS underwriting; and institutional, service and broadcast advertising.

Perception Survey
Focused on the perception of a firm by clients, potential clients and/or a larger community. Often done before developing a new brand, launching a major marketing campaign or in response to changes at a firm.

Podcast
Audio content that can be created by firms to share knowledge and information.

Press List
A list of media outlets that your firm can contact for potential publicity.

Proof Points
Words or phrases that give a specific audience permission to believe a firm's assertion.

Public Domain
Content (in this case, songs) published in 1922 or earlier that is free for public use.

Release Form
A contract signed by an actor or model that gives a firm permission to use their image.

Responsive Design
A website design feature that allows page layout, content, navigation and other features to adjust, scale and move based on the visitor's device.

Royalty-Free
Music that is free to use without fear of copyright infringement.

Scope of Work
The nature of the project. Also, the document that describes the project in terms recognizable by both the client and the A/E/C professional.

Search Engine Optimization (SEO)
The process of improving the visibility of a website or a web page in search engines via natural (unpaid) search results.

Service Advertisements
Highly focused advertisements in which a product or service is described in a selling context to a clearly defined audience.

Shot List
A tracking mechanism to plan and monitor your photography program that includes information about projects to be photographed.

Single-Source Selection
A method of choosing a consultant used when there is one consultant who clearly stands out with the special skills required for the project.

Social Media
The tool set (including blogs, Facebook, Twitter, etc.) which everyone can use to publish content to the Internet. This can include audio, video, photos, text, files, etc.

Social Media Plan
A plan for how a firm will share content via social media.

Special Events
Memorable events put on by a firm that leaves a lasting impression on attendees.

Stock Photography
Pre-existing imagery (as opposed to assignment) that is protected by copyright and may be licensed.

Storyboard
A series of drawings connected by dialogue and directions that outline the shots that you plan to include in a video.

Strengths, Weaknesses, Opportunities, and Threats (SWOT) Analysis
A situational analysis tool that is based on assessing the strengths, weaknesses, opportunities and threats that your firm faces, either as a whole or in a specific market.

Thought Leader
A person or firm who has established themselves as the authority on a topic.

Tombstone Advertisements
Simple, straightforward announcements that are used to announce a significant event like a merger, major personnel change, acquisition or new office.

Trade show
An exhibition for companies serving a specific industry to showcase and demonstrate their products or services. Trade shows are typically sponsored by a professional association and are open to its membership.

Unique Value Proposition
A short statement about a firm's area of expertise that lets prospective clients know what value they'll gain by hiring that firm over another.

Value
1. One of the core beliefs that serve as a guide for a firm's decision making.
2. The worth of a service or product, based on various metrics of measurement.

Video Plan
An outline of the key messages, script and actors to be included in a video, as well as a description of the response the video is intended to elicit from the target audience.

Viral Videos
Videos that are shared at a rapid pace across multiple online and mobile platforms.

Vision Statement
An expression of what a firm aspires to become.

Web Crawlers
Computer programs that browse the Internet in a methodical, automated manner to index website content.

Wire Distribution Service
Services that will broadcast your news release for a fee, giving you access to all of the connections that the service has and allowing you to reach a potentially larger audience.

MARKENDIUM // **Domain 5:** Promotional Activity

13 Related Resources

Brand Architecture:

    Brand Architecture: Concepts and Cases, by R. Harish, 2008

Corporate Identity Guidelines Examples:

    http://www.logodesignlove.com/brand-identity-style-guides

Social Media Monitoring Tools:

    http://blog.hootsuite.com/social-media-monitoring-tools/

Google Keyword Tool:

    http://www.googlekeywordtool.com/

Site Readability Tools:

    http://www.SEO-browser.com

    http://www.logic.com

Popular Media Directories:

    Cision Inc.: http://www.cision.com

    Meltwater Group: http://www.meltwater.com

    Gorkana: http://www.gorkana.com

    My Media Directory: http://www.mymediadirectory.com

    Burrelle's Luce Media Directories: http://www.burrellesluce.com

    The A/E/C Publicity Directory: http://www.fuessler.com/pub.html

    Gebbie All-in-One Directory: http://www.gebbie.com

    Thomson Reuters MyMediaInfo: http://mymediainfo.com/index.html

    Yahoo Media Pages: http://dir.yahoo.com/news_and_media

Stock B-Roll Footage Services:

    http://www.istockphoto.com/footage

    http://www.beachfrontbroll.com

Royalty-Free and Public Domain Music:

    http://www.istockphoto.com/music-clips

http://www.royaltyfreemusic.com

http://www.audiomicro.com/royalty-free-music

http://www.pdinfo.com/public-domain-music-list.php

http://www.pdmusic.org

Stock Photography Services:

http://www.comstock.com

http://www.corbis.com

http://www.creatas.com

http://www.eyewire.punchstock.com

http://www.fotosearch.com

http://www.gettyimages.com

http://www.istockphoto.com

http://www.juniperimages.com

http://www.rubberball.com

http://www.shutterstock.com

14   Figures

pg 9: Identity Map (Marketing Handbook), Figure 2.2a – Marketing Handbook, pg 66

pg 20-22: Social Media Platforms (provided by Mike Reilly)

pg 34: Sample News Release (provided by Marci Thompson)

pg 53: Photo – Marketing Handbook, pg 431

pg 54: Photo – Marketing Handbook, pg 432

pg 56: Photo – Marketing Handbook, pg 429

pg 56: Photo – Marketing Handbook, pg 430

15 Index

301 Redirect 35, 41, 115

A

Advertising Plan 10, 84, 89, 115

Advertorial 55, 57, 115

Analytics 8, 34, 39-41, 115-116

Awards Campaign 83, 115

B

Brand 7, 14-15, 19-22, 33-35, 59, 84, 92, 94, 96, 113, 115-118, 121

Brand Architecture 7, 19-20, 22, 115, 121

Broadcast Advertisements 89, 115

B-Roll 64-66, 115, 121

C

Communications Objectives 7, 23-24, 41, 115

Communications Plan 7, 14, 23-25, 41-42, 50, 112-113, 115

D

Deliverable 64-65, 111, 116

Demographic Characteristics 25-26, 41, 116

Differentiation 14, 17, 22, 42, 116

E

Earned Advertising 88-89, 116

Editorial Calendar 43-44, 48, 52, 57, 85, 116

Exhibit Hall 90, 92, 97, 99, 116

F

Fee-Driven Market 89, 116

G

Google Analytics 34, 39-41, 116

I

Identity Map 7, 17-18, 22, 113, 116, 123

Inbound Marketing 29, 41, 54, 113, 117

Institutional/Image Advertisements 89, 117

Integration 8, 33, 35-36, 41, 117

J

Jury 82-83, 117

K

Keyword 37-38, 41, 117, 121

L

Licensing Agreement 78-79, 117

M

Merit-Driven Market 84, 89, 117

Mission Statement 7, 15-16, 22, 113, 117

Multimedia 9, 58, 66, 112-113, 117

N

Naming Conventions 7, 19-20, 22, 113, 117

News Release 22, 43-49, 57, 117, 120, 123

O

Outbound Marketing 13, 29, 41, 117

Owned Advertising 89, 117

P

Pay-to-Play Advertising 84, 88-89, 117

Perception Survey 15, 22, 113, 118

Podcast 66, 118

Press List 42, 57, 118

Proof Points 21-22, 118

Psychographic Characteristics 25-26, 28, 41, 113

Public Domain 65-66, 118, 121

R

Release Form 65-66, 118

Responsive Design 36, 41, 118

Royalty-Free 65-66, 118, 121-122

S

Scope of Work 11, 13, 107-109, 111, 118

Search Engine Optimization (SEO) 37-39, 41, 45-47, 59, 118, 121

Service Advertisements 89, 118

Shot List 68, 79, 118

Single-Source Selection 108, 111, 118

Social Media 7, 10, 13-14, 23, 28-36, 40-41, 44, 53-54, 58, 62, 66, 85, 87-88, 93, 98, 113, 117-119, 121, 123

Social Media Plan 7, 28, 34, 36, 41, 113, 119

Special Events 10, 13-14, 71, 100-101, 103-104, 106, 119

Stock Photography 64, 67, 71, 78-79, 119, 122

Storyboard 64, 66, 119

SWOT Analysis 17

T

Thought Leader 35, 99, 112, 119

Tombstone Advertisements 10, 87, 89, 119

U

Unique Value Proposition 7, 14, 17, 22, 119

V

Value 2, 7, 14-15, 17, 22, 25, 29, 33, 39, 43, 53, 55, 65-66, 80, 84, 86, 97, 107-108, 119

Video Plan 9, 63, 66, 119

Viral Videos 66, 119

Vision Statement 15-16, 22, 119

W

Web Crawlers 38, 41, 119

Wire Distribution Service 47-48, 57, 120

16   About the Photographer:

Paul Turang is an award-winning photographer who has been photographing architecture and design-related projects for nearly 20 years. Turang and his team have photographed projects throughout the nation. His images have received several international awards and have been featured in a variety of design related publications, including Architectural Record; Buildings: Healthcare Design, Hospitality and Design; Interiors and Sources; Metropolis; LD+A; and others. A member of SMPS Los Angeles, Turang travels regularly for assignments, bringing his passion and vision to leading architecture, design, and construction firms. His website is http://paulturang.com and he can be contacted at paul@paulturang.com.

17   Peer Review:

The following professionals have peer reviewed one or more domains of the MARKENDIUM: The SMPS Body of Knowledge.

Ed Hannan, Executive Editor

Janet Brooks, CPSM
Cynthia Jackson, FSMPS, CPSM
Francis Lippert, FSMPS, CPSM
Fawn Radmanich, CPSM
Julie Shepard, CPSM, ENV SP
Andrea Story, CPSM

DOMAIN 05

18 Body of Knowledge Subject Matter Experts (SMEs)

Dana L. Birkes, APR, FSMPS, CPSM

CMO, Clifford Power Systems, Tulsa, OK

Scott W. Braley, FAIA, FRSA

Principal Consultant, Braley Consulting & Training, Atlanta, GA

Theresa M. Casey, FSMPS, CPSM

Principal, On Target Marketing & Communications LLC, Columbia, CT

Karen O. Courtney, AIA, FSMPS

Chief Marketing Officer, Fanning Howey, Indianapolis, IN

Dana Galvin Lancour, FSMPS, CPSM

Director of Communications, Barton Malow Company, Southfield, MI

Shannah A. Hayley, FSMPS, CPSM

Director of Marketing and Community Engagement, City of Plano, Plano, TX

Linda M. Koch, FSMPS, CPSM

Director of Marketing & Business Development, Pfluger Architects, San Antonio, TX

Michael J. Reilly, FSMPS

Principal, Reilly Communications, Boston, MA

Laurie B. Strickland, FSMPS, CPSM

Director of Marketing, Nitsch Engineering, Boston, MA

Mark Tawara, FSMPS, CPSM

Owner, Manageability, LLC, Kailua, HI

Nancy J. Usrey, FSMPS, CPSM

Associate Vice President, HNTB Design Build, Plano, TX

Andrew J. Weinberg, FSMPS, CPSM

Regional Business Development Manager, Simpson Gumpertz & Heger Inc., New York, NY

Made in the USA
Middletown, DE
24 July 2016